Ross Macdonald

Twayne's United States Authors Series

Warren French, Editor

University of Wales, Swansea

TUSAS 557

ROSS MACDONALD
Photograph courtesy of Alfred A. Knopf, Inc.

Ross Macdonald

By Bernard A. Schopen

St. Anselm College

Twayne Publishers
A Division of G. K. Hall & Co. • *Boston*

9402

Ross Macdonald
Bernard A. Schopen

Copyright 1990 by G. K. Hall & Co.
All rights reserved.
Published by Twayne Publishers
A Division of G. K. Hall & Co.
70 Lincoln Street
Boston, Massachusetts 02111

Copyediting supervised by Barbara Sutton.
Book production by Janet Z. Reynolds.
Book design by Barbara Anderson.

Typeset in 11 pt. Garamond
by Compositors Corporation, Cedar Rapids, Iowa.

Printed on permanent/durable acid-free paper
and bound in the United States of America.

Library of Congress Cataloging-in-Publication Data

Schopen, Bernard.
    Ross Macdonald / Bernard Schopen.
        p.   cm. — (Twayne's United States authors series ; TUSAS 557)
    Includes bibliographical references.
    ISBN 0-8057-7548-X (alk. paper)
    1. Macdonald, Ross, 1915–   —Criticism and interpretation.
I. Title.   II. Series.
PS3525.I486Z86   1990
813'.52—dc20   89–36941
                                                            CIP

To My Parents

Contents

About the Author
Preface
Acknowledgments
Chronology

Chapter One
The Myth of One's Life   1

Chapter Two
The Question of Genre   20

Chapter Three
Searching for Lew Archer   35

Chapter Four
Mastering the Form   51

Chapter Five
The Doomsters   69

Chapter Six
The Legend   83

Chapter Seven
Two Classics   99

Chapter Eight
Underground Art   114

Chapter Nine
The Legacy   126

Notes and References   133
Selected Bibliography   141
Index   147

About the Author

Bernard A. Schopen was born in Deadwood, South Dakota, and attended Black Hills State College, the University of Washington, and the University of Nevada at Reno. He has published essays on John Updike and the American detective novel, as well as a detective novel, *The Big Silence*. He lives with his family in New Hampshire.

Preface

Ross Macdonald's private detective novels have elicited a critical commentary exceeded in volume only by that which addresses the work of Dashiell Hammett and Raymond Chandler. Some of this criticism is quite good, especially insofar as it speaks to the central themes of the novels, but about Macdonald's art most critics have little to say. For some, narrative art seems restricted to the use of language and imagery; for others to the manipulation of what they call "the plot of detection"; for still others to the inclusion of psychomythic materials. The recent essay "The Art of Ross Macdonald" locates Macdonald's artistic merit in the quality of his ideas.[1] I agree with much of what these critics say about these matters, but the matters themselves I do not find to constitute Macdonald's art. Art exists in manner rather than in matter, and narrative art exists not in the ideas or themes a work may develop but in the way they are developed, in the rendering of the patterns of the narration and the relation of these patterns to the effect of the fiction. It is that rendering and effect that I study in the following pages.

Any narrative must "be about" something, of course, and in the tradition of the so-called realistic novel that something has always been human experience. In Ross Macdonald's Lew Archer novels that experience takes place primarily in the rapidly changing society of postwar Southern California as a whole, but also within the narrower confines of familial structures. Macdonald's treatment of this more intimate subject is informed by his own experiences, especially those of his difficult youth; thus, I begin this study by looking at his life and tracing its influence on the central themes of his fiction.

If Macdonald wrote fictions within the essentially realistic tradition, he did so primarily within a specific narrative form—the American detective novel. Because the nature of this genre is so frequently confused, I have found it necessary to introduce my discussion of the novels with an overview of what has also been called the "hardboiled" detective novel. In chapter 2 I define the form, identify the sources of the confusion that perpetually attends critical commentary on it, and place the genre within the broader tradition of the American novel.

In the rest of this study I focus on the art of Ross Macdonald's novels. As he wrote two dozen, however, I could not in a book of this length—and would not in any case—treat them all in detail. I have something to say about each novel, but in most of the individual chapters I deal with a group of novels, most by way of overview, with an extended analysis of one or two that I consider either the best or the most representative. The two exceptions are *The Doomsters* and *The Underground Man*, which I treat at chapter length, the first because it represents the culmination of Macdonald's early work in the Chandlerian tradition and the second because it is the climax of Macdonald's mature art. Macdonald's career demonstrates a clear pattern of artistic development, so I have arranged my discussion chronologically.

I have long enjoyed and admired many of Macdonald's novels, but I come to this study not as a champion but as a critic. My objective is to analyze and evaluate these novels as works of fictional art. I have tried to show which novels are in fact fully realized art and which are not—and why. As to the ultimate "importance" of Ross Macdonald as an American novelist, I make some careful adjudications and what seem to me to be reasonable and modest claims.

Ross Macdonald was not "a major American novelist"[2]—not if that phrase has real meaning—nor do the Lew Archer novels "form a cumulative masterpiece,"[3] and neither Macdonald nor his work benefits from such claims. On the other hand, several of his detective novels are as intellectually and aesthetically satisfying, as emotionally and morally compelling as those of contemporary "mainstream" or "serious" novelists, and we do Ross Macdonald, his novels, and ourselves a disservice by our failure to recognize them as such.

Bernard A. Schopen

St. Anselm College

Acknowledgments

I wish to acknowledge my debt and express my gratitude to the many teachers, colleagues, and friends whose instruction and advice have largely contributed to whatever value this study may have. I especially wish to acknowledge my debt to Ann Ronald, with whom I began discussing Ross Macdonald's work many years ago; to James Cruise, who read a portion of the manuscript; and to William Wilborn and Johann Moser, whose intelligent observations on literature inform many pages of this study.

Above all, I am indebted to Robert Merrill, who read the manuscript in various versions, whose advice was always relevant, and in whom I have found an invaluable reader and constant friend.

Chronology

1915   Kenneth Millar born 13 December in Los Gatos, California, son of John and Anne Millar.

1919   Moves to Vancouver, British Columbia, where his parents separate.

1932   John Millar's death provides money for Kenneth to enroll at University of Western Ontario.

1935   Anne Millar dies.

1938   Kenneth receives A. B. at University of Western Ontario and marries Margaret Sturm; they move to Toronto.

1939   Daughter Linda born.

1941   Margaret Millar publishes her first mystery novel; family moves to Ann Arbor, where Kenneth attends University of Michigan and receives M.A. in 1942.

1944   Kenneth publishes first novel, *The Dark Tunnel,* under his real name; joins U.S. Naval Reserve and serves in Pacific theater.

1946   *Trouble Follows Me* (Kenneth Millar).

1947   *Blue City* (Kenneth Millar).

1948   *The Three Roads* (Kenneth Millar).

1949   First Lew Archer novel, *The Moving Target,* published under pseudonym John Macdonald.

1950   *The Drowning Pool* published under the pseudonym John Ross Macdonald.

1951   *The Way Some People Die* (John Ross Macdonald).

1952   *The Ivory Grin* (John Ross Macdonald); receives Ph.D. with dissertation on Coleridge from University of Michigan.

1953   *Meet Me at the Morgue* (John Ross Macdonald).

1954   *Find a Victim* published with disclosure that "John Ross Macdonald" is Kenneth Millar.

1956   *The Barbarous Coast* published, as all subsequent works will
       be, under pseudonym Ross Macdonald.

1958   *The Doomsters.*

1959   *The Galton Case.*

1960   *The Ferguson Affair.*

1961   *The Wycherly Woman.*

1962   *The Zebra-Striped Hearse.*

1964   *The Chill.*

1965   *The Far Side of the Dollar;* receives Golden Dagger Award in
       Great Britain.

1966   *Black Money; The Moving Target* filmed as *Harper* with
       Paul Newman.

1968   *The Instant Enemy.*

1969   *The Goodbye Look.*

1971   *The Underground Man;* daughter Linda dies.

1974   Receives Grand Master Award from Mystery Writers of
       America.

1976   *The Blue Hammer.*

1977   *Lew Archer, Private Detective* (short stories).

1979   *Self-Portrait: Ceaselessly into the Past* (interviews and essays).

1983   Kenneth Millar dies 11 July in Santa Barbara, California.

Chapter One
The Myth of One's Life

Ross Macdonald wrote no autobiography. This is regrettable, for what he did write and say about his life tantalizes, suggesting far more than it reveals. It is clear, for example, that the events of his childhood haunted him throughout his life; in no discussion of either his life or his work does he fail to remark upon the profound influence of his early years. For all these remarks, however, the details remain vague. Nor do existing secondhand accounts clarify events or fill in gaps. Matthew Bruccoli's critical biography contains little new information about these early years, and while the memoirs of Macdonald's friends provide a strong sense of the character and personality of the adult Ross Macdonald—or, as they knew him, Ken Millar—their discussions of his childhood are restricted to matters that Macdonald himself mentioned. Similarly, while Macdonald often alluded to significant incidents and situations in his adult life, he did not discuss them in any organized or extended fashion.

Thus, the Ross Macdonald that Kenneth Millar chose to show the public remains something of a mystery. He was demonstrably a man of keen intelligence and strong feelings. He was also, on the evidence, a deeply troubled man. He seems to have been a man suspended, in his inner existence, between the forces of twin compulsions. Obsessed with his past, he talked about it, wrote about it in his own voice, and wrote about it in the voice of Lew Archer; at the same time, however, he created and remained behind a reticent reserve, for he was clearly unwilling to make the intimate details of his private life a matter for public discussion. As Ross Macdonald may be said to have hidden behind the figure of Lew Archer, so Kenneth Millar hid behind Ross Macdonald.

As Macdonald himself observed, what he had to say about his life he said in his work. "Most fiction," he once wrote, "is shaped by geography and permeated by autobiography, even when it is trying not to be."[1] This is certainly true of his own fiction. The early novels draw on the experiences of Kenneth Millar as boy and young man, and the later novels are imaginative reworkings of the stuff of his past. His fiction does present two problematic portraits of its author—both impressionistic and ultimately elusive. One is static, a darkly shadowed diorama that takes as its central figure the young Kenneth Millar, an abandoned child and displaced youth who grew to manhood in provincial Canada on the charity of relatives and who appears in the disguise of the troubled and angry young men who frequently occupy the emotional center of the novels. The other is progressive, showing the adult Kenneth Millar, now the novelist Ross Macdonald, engaged in a constant struggle to come to terms with that past; it develops primarily through the fictional maturation of Lew Archer, the narrator of the eighteen detective novels.

Macdonald's acceptance of the victimization of the young Kenneth Millar remained uneasy, as his attitude toward the adults responsible remained ambivalent. In the interviews and occasional pieces that accompanied his late popular and critical success, his discussions of his boyhood are oblique, sometimes cryptic, and always couched in a language that suggests that he had "told a little too much of that story for comfort" (*SP*, 57). A number of times he noted that he had written detective fiction because his material—his early life—was too difficult for him to deal with directly. Early in his career he attempted and failed to write about the experience in his own voice. In mid-career he tried again, only to fall back on Lew Archer. Not long before his death he was considering another attempt to write about the experience without the mediation of Archer and the formal refraction of the detective novel. He did not, perhaps still could not, write that story. What he did write about his childhood, however, suggests why the rest remained unwritten.

Exile to Fifty Rooms: 1915–1933

The writer Ross Macdonald was born Kenneth Millar on 13 December 1915 in Los Gatos, California, the only child of John and Anne Millar, both middle-aged Canadians. Later the family moved to Vancouver, British Columbia, where they remained until 1919, when the Millars separated. ("Separated" is the term Macdonald usually, and charitably, applied to this incident; Bruccoli is less kind: "John abandoned his family without warning.")[2] Mother and son were left destitute in a waterfront boardinghouse; as an adult Macdonald recalled begging for money and food on the streets of Vancouver.[3] Anne Millar, a nurse partially invalided and unable to support her son, moved with him to Ontario, where they shunted between rented rooms and the homes of relatives upon whose charity they depended. When Kenneth was six his desperate mother made plans to put the boy in an orphanage; they had reached the institution's gates before his entreaties dissuaded her. By several accounts, Macdonald never forgot the experience.[4]

For several years Anne and Kenneth lived with relatives, mostly her mother and sisters. A two-year period of stability began when Kenneth was taken in by his aunt and uncle, Beth and Rob Millar; it ended with Beth Millar's death. His father's sister Margaret then sent him to St. John's School, a semimilitary academy in Winnepeg, where he stayed until the stock market crash left his Aunt Margaret unable to afford the tuition. Kenneth was shipped first to an aunt in Medicine Hat, Alberta, and then to Kitchener, Ontario, to live with his maternal grandmother, mother, and another aunt. In 1930 he enrolled in Kitchener-Waterloo Collegiate and Vocational School, graduating two years later. The following year he spent working for room and board on a farm, from which he was ironically rescued by his father's death and an insurance benefit that allowed him to enter college.

Forty years later, describing how he came to write *The Galton Case,* Macdonald summed up both his early experiences and his adult response to them: "My mind had been haunted for years by an imaginary boy whom I recognized as the darker side of my own remembered boyhood. By his sixteenth year he had lived in fifty houses and committed the sin of poverty in each of them. I couldn't think of him without anger and guilt" (*SP,* 51). That imaginary boy, those emotions, and the troubled vision of life that his childhood etched indelibly in his consciousness were to inform all of Macdonald's later work.

Macdonald's memories of an abortive early happiness deepened the bleakness of his later experiences. The brief period in Vancouver, when the family was together, he spoke of with a wistful fondness, alluding only briefly to the "private war" (*SP,* 13) between his parents and focusing instead on several of the "adventures I shared with my father," one of which "still seems the happiest day of my childhood if not my life. I mean the unforgettable day when my father took me to sea in a harbor boat, and I stood beside him in the offshore light, with his hands and my hand on the wheel" (*SP,* 12). It was from this remembered early happiness—Macdonald was not yet four when his father left—that he felt exiled.

Publicly, Macdonald rarely expressed his anger toward the father who deserted him. The anger was there, but it was mitigated by other emotions, for the boy Kenneth came to romanticize John Millar and to identify with him. Macdonald talked proudly of his father's physical strength and intellectual and artistic predilections: "My father had been a swimmer and wrestler, once winner of the two-mile swim across Colpoys Bay; a man of middle size who could lift a half-ton weight. Before he was out of his teens he was teaching school and beginning to write" (*SP,* 12). John Millar, whom his son variously described as a poet, writer, printer, journalist, editor, adventurer, and amateur anthropologist, apparently drifted through the Canadian West as aimlessly as his son was handed from relative to relative within its interior. As the father roamed adventurously, the son was confined within a grim world of marginal poverty dominated by Calvinistic women. Nevertheless, Macdonald said, "I remained my father's son," and his imagination cloaked that father with the raiments of romance: "But east and west he traveled, still on the trail of a wished-for world where Indians and white men shared the unploughed territories or climbed through the blowing passes to the north" (*SP*, 13).

The John Millar whom Macdonald described was, like many of the characters in the novels, a man in pursuit of a dream. This pursuit exiled his son into poverty and humiliation, into what Macdonald called the "deadly game of social Snakes and Ladders which occupied much of my youth" (*SP*, 26), yet both the young Kenneth Millar and the adult Ross Macdonald refused to castigate him—indeed, a defiant pride structures the identification of the son with his father: "My mother and I lived, when we were lucky, on the charity of her mother and her sister. They were good women . . . but in their puritanical household I felt both surrounded and displaced. I was my wandering father's son, after all, and my mother's female relatives could hardly help discerning on my brow the mark of the paternal curse" (*SP*, 31). Beyond that, he felt, the community as a whole placed him under social censure: "People don't attach the same importance to a fatherless boy that they do to one with a father. Their judgments of children depend a great deal on the children's immediate background. In those days, I was my father's son. If I were to turn out well, that would have been a miracle."[5]

After the family broke up, father and son met rarely, "sometimes not for years at a time" (*SP*, 13). Then a series of strokes left the elder Millar an invalid, and he returned to Ontario. Kenneth's emotional confusion intensified; he felt renewed anger, embarrassment at having his father in a hospital charity ward, guilt over his father's helplessness. Still, he continued his idealization of his father. The last time the boy saw his "father's living eyes," John Millar had "lost the power of speech, but he could still write." As Macdonald recounts it, "He wrote me a few lines in a book on his knee. I wish I could tell you what he wrote to me on that day. His writing was so shaky that I couldn't make out the words. But I could see that it was written in rhymed couplets" (*SP*, 14).

If Macdonald's memories centered obsessively on the father who deserted him, they all but ignored the mother who did not. His comments about Anne Millar were few. Long after her death, he said: "We were very close, very good friends, much closer than I realized before she died. She had kept my spirit alive all those years."[6] She also had inculcated in the boy an attitude that increased his sense of alienation from his surroundings: "I'd been taught by my mother from childhood to regard myself as an American."[7] Anne Millar would never let her son forget that he had been born in California, which to her was "'a dream of goodness' to which they would someday prove themselves worthy."[8] The dream of California and Kenneth's sense of exile from it further estranged him from Canada and the puritanical households in which he found himself. Macdonald summed it up in describing the similarities of Kenneth Millar and John Brown of *The Galton Case:* "We shared a sense of displacement, a feeling that, no matter where we were, we were on the alien side of some border. We felt like dubious claimants to a lost inheritance" (*SP,* 32).

His mother also encouraged his ambition, which he subsumed in his interest in writing. Alienation and ambition deepened the boy's uncertainty about his identity and worth, and strengthened his sense that through some cosmic accident or human conspiracy he had been abandoned into circumstances of which he was undeserving and to which he was somehow superior. (*The Galton Case,* the novel in which he first directly addressed these issues, he considered calling "The Castle and the Poorhouse.") Yet this same alienation and ambition led to both Kenneth Millar's taking up residence in Southern California and his transformation into the detective novelist Ross Macdonald.

Before either took place, however, Kenneth Millar made his way through boyhood and youth. In his estrangement, he turned to books. "I was a bookworm. Sometimes I would get up and read a whole book before breakfast."[9] Encountering in *Oliver Twist* fictional situations that paralleled his own, he "read that novel with such intense absorption that my mother feared for my health" (*SP,* 4). Then came his teenage discovery of *The Maltese Falcon,* when "for the first time that I can remember I was consciously experiencing in my own sensibility the direct meeting of art and contemporary actuality" (*SP,* 7). He had begun to write at St. John's Academy, and through high school he continued to produce verse and fiction, and to read: "I was an unwanted guest in the house, and it gradually became a place I only visited when I wanted to sleep. My second home was the public library" (*SP,* 40).

This, then, is the picture of his youth that Macdonald sketched, the "darker side" of his "remembered boyhood" (*SP,* 51). Despite its lack of details, the sketch suggests how his early experiences inform the fiction he later wrote. In fact, Macdonald's description of young Kenneth Millar could serve as an encapsulation of those youthful characters who in the Archer novels so frequently explode to set in motion a chain reaction of destruction and death: "By age 14, I was a conscious undersider. Handed around from uncle to aunt, sent to Sunday school to be hit over the head with Old Testament guilt—fear and wrongdoing—measuring myself against standards I couldn't come up to. . . . There was a sense of illegitimacy. I was in the wrong place and it must be my fault. If the life around you can't contain your own thoughts, you carry guilt and a kind of explosiveness."[10]

But for a few terse remarks,[11] Macdonald offers no evidence that young Kenneth Millar ever allowed his anger to explode into action. And as an adult he was, by all reports, a quiet man, contemplative and carefully spoken, outwardly of a demeanor frequently associated with the professor and scholar that he nearly became. However, his close friends—and they were few, for he was apparently a difficult man to know well—observed evidence of strong emotions carefully confined within his placid exterior. Robert Easton remembered that outwardly Macdonald was "so reserved he seemed rude";[12] at the same time, Easton noted, "there was a dourness and violence in him . . . he was often quick to take offense, irascible, lashing out at injustices real or imaginary. . . . It was as if there were two Kens: one in whom violence and darkness seethed, one yearning for tenderness and light. . . . I sensed the near-presence of that sensitive waif who'd lived in fifty different rooms obliged to accept the charity of others, ever mindful of the orphanage gates and his absent father."[13] Unpurgable, inexpressible in his own voice, the emotions engendered by his youth were instead channeled into his fiction.

From Kenneth Millar to Ross Macdonald: 1933–1956

In 1933 Kenneth Millar enrolled at the University of Western Ontario, where he majored in English and history while continuing to write—his work was published in the university newspaper. Then in 1935 he returned home one day to find his mother dead of a stroke. Depressed, he went to Europe for a year. Upon his return, he reencountered Margaret Sturm, a high school classmate; Macdonald later wrote of this meeting and the resulting events: "I walked into the public library and found Margaret reading Thucydides in Greek. From then on, we saw each other nearly every day. I was just back from Europe, determined to become a writer. Margaret confessed she had the same ambition. We were married in June, 1938, the day after I graduated from college, and honeymooned at summer school in Ann Arbor, where I prepared to become a schoolteacher" (SP, 25).

As with most of what Macdonald wrote about his life, this account is remarkable for what it does not include. Margaret Sturm was not only the best student at Kitchener Institute while Kenneth was there; she was also the mayor's daughter. While they had taken classes together, they had never had a conversation. But Margaret Millar was to write that "his best friend told me years later that Ken said he intended to marry me. Ken's age at the time was fifteen."[14]

The Millars spent the following year in Toronto, where Kenneth took graduate courses at Ontario College of Education. That spring their only child, Linda, was born. At the same time Kenneth Millar became a professional writer. Using a typewriter he had won on a radio quiz program, he wrote "a flock of short stories and sketches for quickly available Toronto markets, most of which were so-called Sunday School papers paying a cent a word. I made over a hundred dollars the first few weeks, and with this blessed wad of cash ransomed my wife and infant daughter out of the Women's College hospital. I was a pro" (*SP*, 30). From 1939 to 1941, while teaching at Kitchener-Waterloo, he continued to write newspaper pieces. Then the publication of Margaret's first mystery novel eased their financial situation, and when he was offered a fellowship at the University of Michigan, the family moved to Ann Arbor.

Professionally, both Margaret and Kenneth thrived at Michigan. She published three more mysteries, and he received his M.A. in 1942 and completed the course work for his doctorate in 1943. In the fall of that year he wrote his first novel, *The Dark Tunnel*. Impetus for this initial effort he credited to Margaret: "By going on and breaking trail, she helped make it possible for me to become a novelist, as perhaps her life with me had helped to make it possible for her" (*SP*, 25). Both Millars benefited from the presence on campus of W. H. Auden in the fall of 1941. Auden knew Margaret's work, and his encouragement, Macdonald said, "marked a point in my life where I chose to become a fiction writer rather than a man who writes about other people's writings as a scholar; that's where I was headed. I would have done both, actually, but this straightened me out and put me on the creative path."[15]

In 1944, after having been turned down the previous year, Kenneth Millar was accepted by the U.S. Naval Reserve and sent to the Pacific and the escort carrier *Shipley Bay* as a communications officer. The same year a spy novel, *The Dark Tunnel*, was published. After the war with Japan ended, the *Shipley Bay* was used as a troop transport, and Millar had time to write his first piece of detective fiction, the short story "Find the Woman," and another spy novel, *Trouble Follows Me*, published in 1946. He was discharged in March 1946, but he did not return to Michigan to complete his degree. Margaret had settled with Linda in Santa Barbara, California, and Kenneth joined them. Except for two brief periods, he lived there the rest of his life.

Between his discharge and the end of 1946, Kenneth Millar wrote two more novels—*Blue City,* a Hammett-like story "about the underlife of an imaginary American city" (*SP,* 26), and a psychological thriller, *The Three Roads.* He then began an autobiographical novel, "Winter Solstice," which effected a minor crisis in his life: "I tried, and got badly bogged down in sloppy feelings and groping prose. I began to doubt my vocation as a writer and my mind turned back toward the comparative safety of graduate school" (*SP,* 35). Before returning to Ann Arbor to complete his Ph.D., however, he wrote a novel narrated by a private detective named Lew Archer.

Of this period Macdonald later wrote, "I was in trouble, and Lew Archer got me out of it" (*SP,* 35). The Archer solution was more complicated and less obvious than Macdonald let on, however. While he was later to write vigorously in defense of the American detective novel, at the time he wrote his first one he was less than committed to the genre. He had long wished to write "serious" or "straight" novels, and when Alfred A. Knopf advised him to put aside the Archer novel, Millar suggested to his agent that it be submitted to other houses pseudonymously. When Knopf then agreed to publish the book under a pseudonym, Millar admitted to his agent, "I am relieved that it is not going to be published under my name."[16] Thus the first Archer novel, *The Moving Target,* came out in 1949 under the name John Macdonald, the first and middle names of Kenneth Millar's father. The dust jacket carried the author's silhouette rather than the standard photograph.

Macdonald's later explanation of the pseudonym—that he took it to avoid confusion with his wife—ignores the facts that Knopf considered the first Archer novel inferior to the work published under the name Kenneth Millar (which is clearly not the case) and that Millar himself then was so uncertain of the novel and its genre that he was inclined to "doubt that I'll be doing any more straight mysteries."[17] Lew Archer certainly got Kenneth Millar out of trouble; the creation of Archer was the first event in Millar's transformation into the detective novelist Ross Macdonald and the first step toward his ultimate artistic achievement. But there is no evidence that he envisioned such a transformation or believed that the critical and popular success he aspired to would result from it.

The Millar family spent the next three years at Ann Arbor, where Kenneth tried to work on "Winter Solstice," taught, and wrote detective fiction. He completed the requirements for his Ph.D. in February 1952. His dissertation, "The Inward Eye: A Revaluation of Coleridge's Psychological Criticism," studied the psychological basis of the critical theory that Coleridge developed in reaction to the positivistic philosophy of his day. Degree in hand, Kenneth Millar did not, however, seek a full-time teaching job. Instead he returned to California and, while he taught part-time at Santa Barbara City College, continued writing.

While Millar was at the University of Michigan, Knopf published *The Moving Target,* which led the crime writer John D. MacDonald to protest the confusion created by Millar's pseudonym. *The Drowning Pool* and *The Way Some People Die,* both written in Ann Arbor, were published under the name John Ross Macdonald; "I don't know where the 'Ross' came from" (*SP,* 39), Macdonald later admitted. Both publisher and author kept the identity of John Ross Macdonald a mystery through publication of the two following novels, *The Ivory Grin* and the non-Archer *Meet Me at the Morgue.* The second and third Archer novels kept the author's silhouette, and the jacket photograph for *Meet Me at the Morgue* was an X-ray of Millar's skull. Finally, both silhouette and skull appeared on the jacket of *Find a Victim,* along with Millar's picture and the announcement that John Ross Macdonald was "no other than KENNETH MILLAR, author in his own name of several notable thrillers and husband of Margaret Millar, another well-known writer of novels of suspense." With *The Barbarous Coast,* published in 1956, Millar abandoned the John, and the author of the Archer novels became to his readers simply Ross Macdonald.

In 1956 Millar completed his transformation to Ross Macdonald in another and more important sense. That year seventeen-year-old Linda Millar was involved in a vehicular homicide, placed on probation, and required to undergo psychiatric treatment. At the same time, as Macdonald later described it, "seismic disturbances occurred in my life. My half-suppressed Canadian years, my whole childhood and youth, rose like a corpse from the bottom of the sea to confront me" (*SP,* 30). The family moved north to Menlo Park, not far from the site of his birth, where Kenneth himself underwent psychotherapy. The novels of Ross Macdonald were never the same thereafter.

Mastery, Triumph, and Tragedy: 1957–1983

While in therapy Macdonald managed to complete another Archer novel, *The Doomsters.* He considered the seventh Archer book to mark "a fairly clean break with the Chandler tradition, which it had taken me some years to digest, and freed me to make my own approach to the crimes and sorrows of life" (*SP,* 120). The novel is that, and considerably more. In *The Doomsters* Macdonald demonstrated that Hammett and Chandler had not permanently fixed the boundaries of the American detective novel, that the form contained additional thematic and aesthetic possibilities. Then, in *The Galton Case,* Macdonald confronted directly the plights and predicaments of his youth. Some of this material had worked its way into earlier novels, but after *The Galton Case* it would be central. That it would take form in the American detective novel was also determined by the eighth Archer novel, for the book established Macdonald's dependence on the mediating voice and vision of private detective Lew Archer. Trying to write the novel that became *The Galton Case*, Ross Macdonald again found himself in trouble; again Lew Archer got him out of it.

In "Writing *The Galton Case*" Macdonald detailed his struggle to transform the stuff of his life in fiction. Trying to write a mainstream novel narrated by the central character, "a boy who recalls aspects of my Canadian boyhood" (*SP,* 53), he found the subject still "too hot" to deal with directly; this led to a decision about narrative perspective as significant as that about material: "A second break-through at the beginning, more technical and less obviously important, came with my decision to use the detective Archer as the narrator. . . . I made up my mind that the convention of the detective novel, in which I had been working for fifteen years, would be able to contain the materials of my most ambitious and personal work so far. I doubt that book could have been written in any other form" (*SP,* 56).

Realizing Archer's importance, Macdonald said that the detective is "the obvious self-projection which holds the eye (my eye as well as the reader's) while more secret selves creep out of the woodwork behind the locked door" (*SP,* 121). The form of the detective novel, as Macdonald was to develop it, does much the same thing, forcing writer and reader to attend to the questions raised by the events while allowing theme to develop through action and pattern rather than through sustained analysis. Except in *The Ferguson Affair,* where as Bruccoli has noted, "nothing particularly important for the novel is gained"[18] with a different narrator and in fact several things are lost, Macdonald never again wrote without his detective narrator.

Macdonald's decision to continue with Archer could not have been an easy one. He had long been unhappy with the reception the Archer books had received from reviewers, readers, and his publishers. This was important economically, for while he and Margaret published regularly, their combined income was about that of a high school teacher. Professionally significant was the fact that neither his editors nor his readers seemed to perceive what Macdonald was doing with the American detective novel and could not appreciate his achievement (Anthony Boucher had been pointing it out in his reviews, but no one was paying attention). Macdonald was both frustrated and depressed. After *The Doomsters* was published he wrote to his editors that he was "giving serious thought to the idea of changing my pace somewhat. . . . I have no desire to expend my powers on a form which does not seem, for one reason and another, to have attained the status I'd hoped for it;

in this country, at least."[19] Feeling that everyone was blinded to the quality of his work by the assumption that Hammett and Chandler had had the last word about what could be done in the form, Macdonald in a moment of frustration elevated himself above both: "They're my masters, sure, but in ways that count to me and a lot of good readers I'd like to sell my books to, I'm beginning to trace concentric rings around those fine old primitives."[20]

Slowly, however, things began to improve. Between 1961 and 1968 Macdonald wrote six Archer novels that in themselves might stand as the most significant body of work in the American detective novel. *The Wycherly Woman, The Zebra-Striped Hearse, The Chill, The Far Side of the Dollar, Black Money,* and *The Instant Enemy* reveal a mastery of both material and form, a fact his readers began to comprehend. During the same period, the Millars' financial situation began to improve. The growth of Macdonald's readership accelerated with the release of the film *Harper,* a retitled version of *The Moving Target* starring Paul Newman, and with the movie money the Millars bought a house in an elite section of Santa Barbara. The movie also generated new interest in Macdonald's previous work, and Bantam began republishing the earlier novels in paperback. Critical attention to the Archer novels also increased. If neither the readership nor the criticism was as extensive as Macdonald desired, each was superior to what the two previous decades had seen.

This period brought personal difficulties, however. In May of 1959, Linda Millar, then a student at the University of California at Davis, disappeared. Her father hired detectives, made appeals on radio and television, and sent messages through the press. Nearly two weeks later she was located in Reno, safe and unharmed but with no recollection of where she had been. Afterwards Macdonald was hospitalized with hypertension. He also suffered from gout, attacks of which he warded off with long walks.

By and large, the 1960s were good for Macdonald. He lived comfortably if frugally and quietly—swimming almost daily in the Pacific, birdwatching, and involving himself in local environmental matters—while steadily producing Lew Archer novels, which just as steadily increased his readership, income, and reputation. Blurb writers and reviewers had long since established his position in the triumvirate of American detective novelists; pronouncements about "the tradition of Hammett, Chandler, and Macdonald" became commonplace. Then in 1969 Macdonald achieved with his twenty-first novel what he had labored after for twenty-five years: an immense popular, critical, and financial success.

John Leonard has amusingly described the "literary conspiracy" that resulted in a review of *The Goodbye Look* on the front page of the *New York*

Times Book Review.[21] In that review William Goldman, the novelist and screenwriter who had written the script for *Harper,* declared the Archer novels "the finest series of detective novels ever written by an American,"[22] and in a tag piece Leonard asserted that with *The Galton Case* ten years before Macdonald had "turned into a major American novelist."[23] *The Goodbye Look* made the *Times* best-seller list, where it remained for over three months, and went through eight printings. At the same time Bantam began reprinting all of Macdonald's novels in paperback. At fifty-three Macdonald had "broken through" into the national consciousness.

In November of 1970 the Millars' daughter, now married and the mother of a son, died of a cerebral accident. Despite his grief and the distractions of fame, Macdonald completed *The Underground Man,* which was reviewed by Eudora Welty on the front page of the *New York Times Book Review,* prompted a *Newsweek* cover story, and also became an immediate best-seller. So did the novel that followed, *Sleeping Beauty. The Blue Hammer,* his twenty-fourth and, as it turned out, last novel, also sold well.

The 1970s were a decade of unqualified professional triumph for Macdonald. His new novels were well received by both reviewers and readers. Articles about the Archer novels began to appear in literary and scholarly journals, and two book-length studies of his work were published. In 1974 he received the Grand Master Award of the Mystery Writers of America. His financial condition improved even more with the film version of *The Drowning Pool* (again starring Paul Newman) and on network television a production of *The Underground Man* and a series based on Lew Archer stories.

While in the 1970s Macdonald reaped the professional fruits of his long labor, the decade brought more personal problems, which only began with the death of his daughter. Early in the decade, Margaret Millar was diagnosed as suffering from oracular degeneration, which four surgeries failed to retard; by 1982 she was legally blind, able "to see where I'm going and that's about all."[24] Then in the latter half of the decade Macdonald began to suffer bouts of confusion. These grew more severe. As his wife described it, "Ken has always been slow and quiet. I noticed that he was slower and quieter all of a sudden, and odd things began to happen."[25] Others noticed the change. Julian Symonds has recalled the 1978 world crime writer's conference in New York, at which Macdonald "made a speech, the early part of which was uttered rather as though he were talking to himself, with no audience in mind. The effect was odd, but seemed attributable to his public shyness."[26] The diagnosis was Alzheimer's disease, untreatable premature senility.

Macdonald's condition deteriorated slowly but inexorably. By 1982 he still had moments of lucidity, but Margaret observed that "he knows what is happening to him, but he doesn't really feel things."[27] The last public glimpse of Ross Macdonald is Wayne Warga's 1982 interview with Margaret for the *Los Angeles Times* upon the publication of her novel *The Murder of Miranda*. Her husband was with her, for she had not left him alone for several years and had been carefully shielding him from the curious and the ignorant. This final view of Ross Macdonald is tinged with tragedy. Margaret sits with her husband of over forty years and speaks of their present life: "Here we are, two people who live by books. What has happened has taken 90% of our lives away. . . . He loves to move his books around. He loves his books." At this her silent husband "smiles, nods and picks up the thread of his wife's conversation, 'We're like bookends,' he says. 'She's very protective of me. Which is nice.' He does not speak again."[28]

Nor would either Ross Macdonald or his private detective Lew Archer speak again. Kenneth Millar died 11 July 1983.

Life into Art

Ross Macdonald spoke and wrote frequently about the relation of his life to his fiction. That relation, however, has been misconstrued by many interviewers and critics. Certainly it is misleading to assert that "Macdonald asked to be read autobiographically."[29] Ross Macdonald specifically pointed out that he wrote not *about* his early life but *from* it, that no character in the canon is a fictionalized version of Kenneth Millar. Even John Brown, the young man in *The Galton Case* whose early life in many respects resembles his own, he described as "an imaginary boy" who haunted the "darker side" of his remembered childhood. It was not himself that Macdonald wrote about; he wrote about fictional characters enmeshed in a reality that "accurately reflects the vision of the world which my adult imagination inherited from my childhood" (*SP*, 51). And while it is true that, as Bruccoli has pointed out, "the figure of Linda Millar can be perceived behind the troubled girls in her father's novels,"[30] the first of these disturbed young women appears in *The Drowning Pool*, which was published when Linda Millar was ten years old. Macdonald himself established the proper relation of his life and art: "You don't write about your own life, but you derive the shapes of your fiction from your own life—sort of make a myth out of your own life."[31] Beyond that, no one character in his novels represents the author: "As I write a book . . . my ego is dispersed through several characters, including usually some of the undesirable ones, and I am involved with them to the limit of my imaginative strength" (*SP*, 56).

Nevertheless, Kenneth Millar's experience contributes to all of

Macdonald's work and clearly informs the later novels. The general subject of his novels, Macdonald said, "is evil. All mystery novels are about evil."[32] In his fiction, evil results from two distinct but related conditions. The first, perhaps the psychic residue of his early fundamentalist religious training and the naturalistic fiction he avidly read, is that collection of predeterminations we indicate by the term *fate*. The notion runs through all the novels, finding its clearest expression in the last: fate is the "place and time and family you're born into."[33] The second is "human error."[34] Sometimes Archer traces the evil to its source in a human choice; sometimes he loses the trail in the tangle of time or the confusion of motive. But in the novels he narrates, evil for the most part is what the characters *do,* not what they *are*.

As most commentators have noted, the evil that the characters do occurs within the confines and context of Macdonald's more specific subject: the moral, psychological, and emotional dynamics of the family. In Macdonald's fiction the thematic link between evil and the family, between human error and human suffering, is intricate, complex, and subtle. Families are afflicted and often destroyed by evil, but it is an evil for which at least one member of that family is usually responsible. Often that character is of a preceding generation, for in these novels the past is always powerfully part of the present. The later novels especially manifest a clear temporal structure: a generation ago someone committed a crime—usually murder, the "objective correlative . . . to spiritual death";[35] although the crime remains unsolved, or even undetected, it has psychological ramifications that infect human minds and hearts; these, after years of poisoning a family with psychoemotional toxins, cause a sudden eruption of violence and misery. Enter Archer. His investigation begins in the present, twists back into the past, threads together then and now as his inquiry into crime becomes an examination of character, his consideration of the present an assessment of the past, his dismantling of a family's facade of respectability an exposure of the human evil at its foundation.

As Macdonald observed, Archer's "explorations are essentially of people and their lives rather than of terrain and clues. He's a psychological and moral detective."[36] The combination in Macdonald's novels of the psychological nature of evil and their thematic focus on the family has led most critics to the Oedipus legend—both the Sophoclean and Freudian versions—for interpretive guidance. Macdonald acknowledged Freud's influence in a sentence that critics often quote, pointing out that "Freud deepened our moral vision and rendered it forever ambivalent." But the entire passage needs to be cited if Macdonald's view is not to be misrepresented: "While psychoanalysis and related disciplines have influenced my thinking, profoundly I hope, the final sources of my particular vision, an articulated vision of pity and terror, are found in traditional literature from Sophocles to Kafka. Freud deepened the grounds of our moral vision and rendered it forever ambivalent, but it was Shakespeare who wrote: 'The gods are just, and of our pleasant vices make instruments to plague us.'"[37]

While they make use of Freud, the novels are not fictionalized versions of psychoanalytical theory; neither are they a retelling of the Oedipus legend, for all the prominence of the exile-and-return pattern. Even more to the point, as Edward Margolies has perceived, the novels' recurring pattern of an internecine violence engendered by the crimes of a previous generation suggests a sensibility "as much Aeschylian as it is Oedipal."[38]

In Ross Macdonald's fictional world, evil crystallizes in human hearts as desire and aspiration compress under the pressures of emotional, psychological, and social forces over which the individual often has little control. Consequently, the moral implications of the action are frequently ambivalent, if not ambiguous. Characters are clearly responsible for their actions, and for the suffering and sorrow they inflict on those around them. The cause of these actions, however, is rarely simple; more often it lies deep in the past, in a choice or act or event from which spins a complex psychosocial web of deceit and desire. Most often the ultimate cause of evil in Macdonald's novels is love.

Again and again the mystery that Lew Archer must solve is the mystery of love. The families he investigates are created by love. Through love they are conceived and born and nurtured; perhaps more than blood, love binds them together, makes them families. In Macdonald's fiction, however, love also maims, cripples, and destroys families. In the Archer novels, love is often the primary agent of the action and the dynamic force in the central thematic patterns. Exile and return, the search for the father, the quest for identity—these and other motifs that Macdonald transposed from his life to his fiction have at their core the desire for love, for the security that comes of being loved and the identity that comes of loving. In the later novels, the basic motivation of the troubled adolescents whose acts set the plot in motion is a real or perceived lack of love. But while lack of love creates trauma, loving and being loved frequently wreak havoc. Most of the crimes in the novels result from the imperatives of sexual love, and many of the criminal psyches have been warped by an oppressive and restrictive parental love. Macdonald's characters suffer from love, from its presence and its absence. Some of them die because of it, but rarely do they die for it—Mark Blackwell in *The Zebra-Striped Hearse* being one obvious exception. And over and over again, they kill for it.

Macdonald's investigation into the nature of love reveals the ambiguities that he finds lurking within this elemental human emotion. In his fiction, love is a swirl of antithetical impulses and conflicting desires. Sometimes it is yoked with its opposite; in both *The Ferguson Affair* and *Sleeping Beauty* characters quote Catullus: "Odi et amo." Invariably love is colored by other feelings—shades of loneliness or alienation, tints of ambition or greed, streaks of anger or lust. Often it provides a means of self-deception or the exercise of power. Neither it nor the moral condition of the characters who love is ever simple. In Macdonald's fiction there are few "good" characters, few "bad." Characters love as they do not because they pervert a pure and godly emotion but because they partake of the human condition. Macdonald neither accuses nor condemns them. His evaluations are rigorously moral, to be sure, but they are decidedly not moralistic. Lew Archer's judgments, of course, are frequently moralistic; but as his creator pointed out and the novels confirm, Archer's moral comments "reflect my attitudes (but deeper attitudes remain implicit)" (*SP*, 121).

Still, Archer is central to the moral assessments in the novels he narrates. His observations inform us of the nature of the other characters, his perceptions guide us to the significance of their attitudes, actions, and emotions, and his own attitudes, actions, and emotions direct us to the proper view of the other characters and the meaning of their stories. All of this is complicated by the fact that Archer himself shares many of the problems and dilemmas of the people he investigates. He carries with him his own ghosts—a troubled and violent adolescence, a broken marriage—and he confronts his own loneliness, acts from his own compulsions, makes his own mistakes. He is, as Macdonald said, "not a model of morality, but . . . he's a better man than most of the people he has to work with. . . . He's not a moral ideal, not a paragon, but a guy that is fairly trustworthy."[39]

In many ways a compelling figure, Archer has received considerable and largely approving attention from Macdonald's critics. Typical is Jacques Barzun's contention that Archer "is a private detective whose concern with society no less than his integrity and investigative skill make him a figure to believe in and admire."[40] Much is made of the later Archer's compassion and compulsive caring, less of the anger and inclination to violence of the Archer in the early novels. Of what lies behind Archer's responses, of course, we know little. He speaks of his experiences outside the novels only in brief remarks scattered through the canon. Still, so favorably has his detective struck readers that Macdonald found it necessary to repeat that Archer, as he once put it, "is not the main object of my interest, nor the character with whose fate I am most concerned" (*SP*, 57).

Nor is Lew Archer the fictional embodiment of his creator. That Archer early and late shares some of the attitudes and feelings of his creator is unquestionable; that these are of import in interpreting the individual novels is dubious. The nature of Macdonald's identification with his narrator has been, I believe, largely misunderstood. His frequently cited remark that "Archer was created from the inside out. I wasn't Archer, exactly, but Archer was me," for example, nearly always omits the observation that precedes it and establishes its context: "I tried to explain that while I had known some excellent detectives and watched them work . . . "(*SP,*113). Archer, that is, was not a fictionalized version of a real detective but an imaginative creation, not a fantasized version of the author but a projection of specific authorial qualities onto a specific fictional character. And Macdonald's assertion that Archer is a "deliberately narrowed version of *the writing self*" (my emphasis) comments on his function as narrator. To take Archer as the authorial voice in the novels he narrates is to misread them. Several of the novels, in fact, are constructed so as to modify or refute Archer's conclusions. As Macdonald insisted, he is "better represented by the whole book than by any one of its characters" (*SP,* 53).

For all his interest as a character, Archer was to his creator more important as a fictional device. On the one hand, he functioned as "a welder's mask which enables both writer and reader to handle dangerously hot materials" (*SP,* 3); on the other, he served as a vehicle that could convey both author and reader through the various levels of society. The second is as important to Macdonald's purposes as the first, for if the family and its failures is his primary subject, that subject has social ramifications. As families spread over generations, they also often spread through various layers of a society stratified, in America, by money. In the Archer novels wealth separates as love and blood unite, and Archer's investigations reveal not merely the guilt of individuals but the "relationships between various members of a society and the various levels of society."[41] Archer moves over the social landscape, charting the fissures through which violence has erupted, mapping the human and familial fault lines that run through the economically determined classes of "classless" American society.

In the Lew Archer novels, that society is specific to postwar Southern California. Los Angeles and its environs has of course featured prominently in twentieth-century American fiction as both setting and subject. For novelists from Nathanael West and Aldous Huxley to Joan Didion and Thomas Pynchon, Southern California has served as a microcosm of America, an example of its moral failings and spiritual ills, a symbolic manifestation of the corruption of its own symbolic version of itself—the American dream. But the thirty years that Macdonald chronicled was of special significance. A period of explosive population growth and burgeoning affluence, the years be-

tween 1945 and 1975 saw Southern California become the cultural bell-
wether of the country. From children's fads to political movements, what was
to happen in America usually happened first in Southern California. Little of
this appears directly in Macdonald's fiction, at least in the manner that someone like Robert B. Parker was to later describe American cultural trends down
to the brand names. What pervades the novels is rather the set of attitudes
and assumptions that pervade the society in which they are set, the felt reality
of the period.

"Here in California," Macdonald said, "what you've got is an instant meg-
alopolis superimposed on a background which could almost be described as
raw nature. What we've got is the twentieth century right up against the
primitive."[42] What we've got in Macdonald's fiction is an instant society
made up largely of immigrants from other parts of the country who have
come to California in the hope of fulfilling their own versions of the American dream. Rare is the Archer novel in which one or more of the central characters does not come from the Midwest. In the Californian society that they at
once belong to and create, the twentieth century and its material and techno-
logical trappings are little more than a thin veneer over the primitive emotions and dreams of its members. As the "last frontier," Southern California
has also been the last opportunity to start over, to live a life dictated by inner
aspiration rather than cultural heritage, to be what one would be rather than
what society and custom and family would have one be. But as the home of
Hollywood and The Great American Dream Machine, it is a construct of artifice and illusion; the society in which one can become whatever he chooses is
populated with people who are not what they seem. "Life in California does
have a fairytale aspect. It seems unreal unless you get into the interior of it.
Unless you really understand how people are living here, it looks like a
dream."[43] It is a dream that people will sometimes kill to maintain. When
they do, Archer must investigate both the dream and the dreamers. Invariably what he discovers is not dream but nightmare. For if dreams liberate the
individual from social and familial restraints, they remove his obligations to
honor the restrictions and injunctions of traditional moral systems. Thus the
liberation of the individual results in social chaos.

"The essential problem," Macdonald once observed, "is how you are going
to maintain values, and express values in your actions, when the values aren't
there in the society around you, as they are in traditional societies. In a sense,
you have to make yourself up as you go along."[44] He offers no solution to this
problem, as he provides no correctives to the moral failings of his characters.
He aspires simply to understand: "We all suffer terrible losses, we all go
through the troubles of life. The purpose of art is to put them in a context so

we can see not just the troubles but the meaning of them, where they came from and where they lead. It isn't sorrow and trouble we can't stand, but meaningless sorrow, trouble that leads nowhere" (*SP,* 45–6). While "in general, the Archer books could be called hopeful,"[45] for Macdonald himself, as he strove in novel after novel to come to understand, to accept, to forgive his past, the primary consolation was the consolation of art.

In its mature form, that art is eminently satisfying. Intricate, subtle, crackling with energy and ribbed with causality, the Archer novels yield manifold pleasures. As detective novels they lead the reader through a dark, mysterious world of violence, carefully modulating anticipation and revelation into a structure of suspense. As novels of character, they probe the recesses of the human heart, exposing illusion and delusion and confusion, silent suffering and seething anger and haunting fear, good and evil. And as works of narrative art they create elaborate patterns of character and scene, impulse and incident, image and symbol—patterns that at once reveal and reinforce meaning.

The meaning of Ross Macdonald's art is the meaning of his life. "A man's fiction," he once wrote, "no matter how remote it may seem to be from the realistic or the autobiographical, is very much the record of his particular life" (*SP,* 5). But writing is also an act of communication, and what Macdonald's fiction communicates is something larger than the personal. It does precisely what he said all fiction does that is written for a large and multilayered audience. The Archer novels dramatize and criticize the confrontations of contemporary values at the same time that they embed the spoken language in the written documents of the culture; they also, as he said of all good fiction, hold "us still and contemplative for a moment, caught like potential shoplifters who see their own furtive images in a scanning mirror, and wonder if the store detective is looking" (*SP,* 9).

Chapter Two
The Question of Genre

The 1971 publication of *The Underground Man*, Ross Macdonald's sixteenth Lew Archer book, effected a critical response unprecedented for a detective novel. Eudora Welty, on the front page of the *New York Times Book Review*, hailed it as a "stunning achievement" and insisted that "in our day it is for such a novel as *The Underground Man* that the detective form exists."[1] Walter Clemons followed with an equally laudatory review for "one our best novelists,"[2] and in a *Newsweek* cover story Raymond A. Sokoloff opined that Macdonald had "pushed beyond the conventional limits of his genre" and made "literature out of the thriller form."[3] Soon, however, voices arose to dispute these claims. Richard Schickel argued that "Macdonald's reputation is at the moment in process of gross inflation,"[4] and Bruce Cook accused Macdonald of "mangling the form."[5] G. A. Finch complained that since Macdonald's "election to the ranks of 'serious writers'" his work had deteriorated because of what Finch construed to be "a displacement of the guaranteed built-in satisfactions of the private eye mystery."[6] And Geoffrey Hartman, while noting Macdonald's virtues as a novelist, nevertheless asserted that the "voracious formalism" of the detective novel precludes any work in the genre from achieving the status of "high" literature.[7]

T. R. Steiner has summed up this dispute over Macdonald and his work as "yesterday's news": "In bringing him to national prominence, his promoters over-stated his stature, so the debunking was predictable. Although many of the criticisms were valid, as many were overly harsh, uninformed or just plain wrong."[8] Steiner's description of the pattern of claim and counterclaim is certainly accurate; the debate is far from over, however, for the issues implicit in it remain in the critical air. The controversy in fact had little to do with either *The Underground Man* or Macdonald's extensive body of work; it resulted, rather, from the unstated assumptions and begged questions on both sides. Regrettably, this tendency toward easy assertions continues to confuse much of the commentary on detective fiction.

Sokoloff observed that "detective fiction has always been a neglected step-child of literature,"[9] and despite a proliferation of academic studies over the last two decades, such is still the case. While a few essays about detective novels have appeared in major journals, and a few journals have devoted issues to detective fiction,[10] most criticism of the genre continues to appear in publications specializing in either mystery fiction or popular culture. Perhaps understandably, this criticism has been little inclined to employ with precision the terms that confuse the debate over *The Underground Man* and Ross Macdonald's status as a novelist. Thus, the real questions remain. What is the detective novel of the sort that Macdonald wrote? Is it generically of a piece with the mystery, the thriller, the suspense story? Is it, with its roots in popular culture, radically and irremediably lowbrow? Do its formal conventions prevent it from reaching a level of significant fictional achievement? Can a detective novel be a serious novel? What makes a novel "serious," or "art," or "literature"? What in fact do these words we toss around so casually actually mean?

Genre and the "Plot of Detection"

E. D. Hirsch, Jr., has argued that most interpretive disputes result from "a disagreement about genre."[11] This is certainly the case with those surrounding Macdonald's work. Discussion of detective novels is disputatious because critics place in a single category any fiction with an element of mystery or suspense or "detection." For example, a recent volume of essays on "detective fiction" announces on its paperback cover that it treats "works by Agatha Christie, Ian Fleming, Raymond Chandler, Dashiell Hammett, Ross Macdonald, John le Carré, and other master mystery writers."[12] This elision of generic demarcations is not without its critical rationalization. A recent version has all novels of "suspense or detection" as variations of a "bare formula: there is always *a hunter, a hunted, a reason for the hunt*, and *a victim*."[13] The problem with this sort of reductionism, however, is that this "formula" is so "bare" as to be meaningless. The "hunt" schematic applies as well to *Heart of Darkness, Les Misérables*, and *Track of the Cat*, as well as to most of Dickens and much of Hardy and Faulkner, but it requires an audacious thesis-mongering to see these as "novels of suspense and detection." On the other hand, in le Carré's *The Little Drummer Girl*, who is the hunter and who is the hunted, what is the reason for the hunt and who is the victim? To ask these questions of the novel's theme is to expose the ambiguities and paradoxes at its heart. To ask them as matters of a narrative "formula" is to approach incoherence.

Unfortunately, incoherence invariably results when this approach, which identifies the generic with the formulaic, is taken to its logical end. Thus the consideration of formula becomes the establishment of absolute patterns, the delineation of conventions the codification of requirements. Thus both writers and readers of detective novels try to impose rules on the genre.[14] Thus one critic insists that the type of novel Macdonald wrote will have as its "major components . . . the waste-land landscape, the quest motif, and the hard-drinking detective."[15] Thus another seriously finds fault with *The Underground Man* because "Archer seems not to have an office . . . and not once is he threatened with loss of his license."[16]

Noticeably absent from these discussions is an acknowledgment of what readers immediately perceive about the novels of, for example, Agatha Christie, Ian Fleming, and Raymond Chandler—that is, not the subtle similarities but the obvious differences. In fact, novels featuring Hercule Poirot, James Bond, and Philip Marlowe differ so radically as to be essentially incomparable. Critics like John Cawelti and George Grella, whose studies are among the best we have,[17] distinguish the "formal" or "British" or "classical" detective novel from the "hardboiled" or "American," and these from the spy novel; both critics, however, find a common "plot of detection" in these works, and they organize much of their discussions around it. But the plot of detection that critics would find common to the fictions does not exist. What does exist are two distinctly different plot structures created by different means for different aesthetic purposes.

In his excellent discussion of these two plots, Timothy Steele has cogently demonstrated that the plot of detection as it was developed by Edgar Allan Poe, the acknowledged father of detective fiction, arises from a rigid and restrictive aesthetic. Under the sway of German Idealism and an "art for art's sake" philosophy, Poe theorized a literature designed to produce a preconceived aesthetic effect, to which all elements of the work are subordinate. According to Poe, the artist works out an abstract design for his fiction and then selects as "material" whatever accommodates that design. Plot, both in theory and in Poe's fiction, is an abstract and mechanical construct of events. Characters are mere agents of plot, and serious human and moral concerns are incidental to the primary purpose of the fiction. As Steele observes, "in no place does Poe suggest relating the material or the effect to some direct existential knowledge of life."[18] This concept of the plot of detection has not simply been accepted by writers of formal detective stories; it has been insisted upon. Writers from Dorothy Sayers to Jacques Barzun have maintained that in the detective novel there is no place for "the human element." As Barzun said, "the tale does not pretend to social significance nor does it probe the depths of the soul. The characters it presents are not persons but types, as in the gospels: the servant, the rich man, the camel driver (now a chauffeur)."[19] The desired effect is always the ratiocinative solving of a logical puzzle, to which serious questions about the nature of society or the propriety of human conduct are irrelevant or, if they appear in the fiction, ultimately destructive. In contrast to Poe's mechanical notion of plot Steele places that of Aristotle. Aristotle values plot above character because he believes that action determines character, because "human life is most richly revealed in action and because it is by means of plot that the dramatist represents action."[20] For Aristotle, a fiction is an imitation of a human action; the emphasis, of course, is as much on "human" as on "action," for Aristotle perceived character as expressing attitudes toward certain fundamental human questions. The relation of plot and character to questions of morality and values is, as Steele notes, crucial to any generic consideration of detective fiction: "Aristotle, then, viewed plot not just as a contrivance, but in relation to broader problems of life and literature. Many writers and critics of detective fiction, in contrast, have tended to regard plot wholly as an end in itself."[21]

And where does Steele find the expression of the Aristotelian concept of plot? In Raymond Chandler's assertion that the detective novel should "consist of plausible actions of plausible people in plausible circumstances."[22] But Chandler here simply echoes the remarks of Joseph Shaw, editor of the pulp magazine *Black Mask*, in which both Chandler and Hammett published their first detective stories. Shaw insisted that "action is meaningless unless it involves recognizable human character in three-dimensional form."[23]

To suggest, then, that the novels of Agatha Christie and Raymond Chandler share a common plot of detection is to reduce the concept of plot to an abstraction of so little value that discussions based on it risk descending into gibberish. Beyond that, it ignores what most readers immediately perceive— that the novels of writers like Dashiell Hammett and Raymond Chandler and Ross Macdonald are of such ontological similarity that they can be discussed meaningfully only as a separate category of fiction.

The American Detective Novel

As Lucy pointed out to Snoopy in a *Peanuts* cartoon, the phrase "in the tradition of Hammett, Chandler, and Macdonald" has become a cliché for reviewers and advertisers of a particular type of detective novel. This testifies both to the obvious formal singularity of these novels and to the manifest superiority of the work of Hammett, Chandler, and Macdonald to that of others in the genre. These three writers constitute a "tradition" in the Leavisian sense—"the major writers who count"[24]—within the larger tradition of what has come to be called the "hardboiled" or "American" detective novel. And it is within this quintessentially American tradition—which derives from Cooper, Crane, Hemingway, and Fitzgerald rather than from Poe and Conan Doyle—that the novels of Ross Macdonald reside.

Most commentators on the American detective novel are aware of the circumstances of its first appearance. As Cawelti observes, "in the early 1920s there emerged a detective story formula so different from the classical genre that it constituted a distinctive type."[25] The form arose in the "pulps," inexpensive magazines containing western, mystery, sporting, and adventure stories written for an unsophisticated male audience. What was to become the American detective novel began in stories that combined elements of the detective story with the hero and the thematic concerns of that other quintessential American form, the western. By moving the frontier hero and his American attitudes into the city and the present, the pulp writers unknowingly created a genre that proved particularly relevant to the human issues and problems of twentieth-century American life and at the same time critical of the organized human environment—American society—in which these issues and problems developed.

Cawelti found of particular importance in this new fiction two modifications of the older detective form: "the subordination of the drama of solution to the detective's quest for the discovery and accomplishment of justice; and the substitution of a pattern of intimidation and temptation of the hero for the elaborate development in the classical story of what Northrop Frye calls 'the wavering finger of suspicion' passing across a series of potential suspects."[26] Cawelti's first modification points to the specific function of the "detection element" in the American detective novel. Solution of the mystery is not the primary purpose of these fictions; rather, it is the means by which the novelist achieves a detailed examination of the relationship between character and society. Thus from the beginning the dramatic purpose of the form has been the exploration of human and moral themes. But when Cawelti identifies the action of the American detective novel with the "quest" archetype and its "pattern of intimidation and temptation" of the detective, he roots the form in tales of knight-errantry. Grella also sees it thus: "Chivalric romance serves a more than incidental function, providing not only a hero, but narrative structure and moral judgment as well."[27]

While this perhaps applies to Chandler's work, it does not pertain to that of Hammett and Macdonald. In fact, Grella himself identified the true forebears of the private detective, finding them not in medieval romance but in classic American fiction: "Though superficially an altogether new kind of folk hero, the private detective is actually another avatar of that prototypical American hero, Natty Bumppo. . . . Like the lonely man of the forest, he

works outside the established social code, preferring his own instinctive justice to the often tarnished justice of civilization."[28]

Operating on the edge of a society from which he is estranged, the detective—"private" rather than "official"—is in this new form a solitary figure:
"Finding the social contract vicious and debilitating, he generally isolates
himself from normal human relationships. His characteristic toughness and
his redeeming moral strength conflict with the values of his civilization and
cause him, like Natty Bumppo or Huckleberry Finn, to flee the society
which menaces his personal integrity and spiritual freedom."[29] Yet because
there is no longer a frontier to which he can flee, a territory for which he can
"light out," the detective must remain in contact with his society. He does so
through his work. As he goes about this work, Cawelti notes, he "sets out to
investigate a crime but invariably finds that he must go beyond the solution
to some kind of personal choice or action. . . . We find the detective forced to
define his own concept of morality and justice, frequently in conflict with the
social authority of the police."[30]

Implicit in the assessments of both Cawelti and Grella is the problematic
relation of the detective to his society. He is not its representative. Often he
is the antagonist of its official agents, and just as often his investigation reveals the inability of social organizations to deal with the real problems of
human existence. The American detective novel is, like much American fiction, critical of society to the point that it approaches the antisocial. Histori-
cally, it has also been essentially antifemale. As many critics have noted,
much of the fiction deemed intrinsically American expresses hostility toward women; as feminist critics have observed, this fiction views women as
a threat to masculine hegemony. Consistently in these works women are
dressed in the cloth of male dreams and, when those dreams are destroyed
by "reality," accused of treachery.[31] In much the same way the hardboiled
detective novel borders on—and in the work of writers like Mickey Spillane
crosses the border into—misogyny.

I am arguing that the American detective novel takes part of its generic
definition from its manifestation of attitudes that critics have long found to
constitute a unique "Americanness." By this I do not suggest that the genre is
available only to American writers, although by and large only Americans
have written successfully in it. Rather, I refer to the ideological qualities it
shares with those fictions that make up *a,* if not *the,* dominant strain in the
American novel. The canon shifts, of course, but since the turn of the century
it has foregrounded a fiction marked by the specific nature of the relation between a hero-protagonist and his society. The masculine pronoun here is deliberate. By and about American men, these novels all say roughly the same

thing about the experience of being an American male, about his relation to females, and about his stance toward his native society.

Nina Baym has cogently argued that the "classic" American novel is the creation of male critics from Vernon Parrington to Richard Poirier. The fact remains, however, that the writers whom these critics have identified as uniquely American—Cooper, Hawthorne, Melville, Twain, Hemingway, Fitzgerald, Faulkner—are, if not the creators of a unique American vision, certainly major American writers. And their novels present a uniform view of the masculine American experience, a view that, Baym observes, "narrates a confrontation of the American individual, the pure American self divorced from specific social circumstances, with the promise offered by the idea of America. . . . The myth also holds that, as something artificial and secondary to human nature, society exerts an unmitigatedly destructive pressure on individuality."[32] As Baym also notes, in these novels society is "represented with particular urgency in the figure of one or more women."[33]

It is simply a fact that this "classic" American fiction is dominated by a view of the relations between men and women as threatening to and potentially destructive of men. In this fiction, the male protagonists either flee women and the society they are thought to represent—Huck Finn's lighting out for the territory is paradigmatic—or embrace women only to have their dreams and sometimes their lives destroyed—here the paradigm is Jay Gatsby.

This view dominates the American detective novel as well. Since Sam Spade turned Brigid O'Shaughnessy over to the police, the hardboiled detective novel has focused on the relations between men and women, valorizing the male desire for both sexual possession of the female and independence from the socializing impulse she is thought to embody. This valorization takes place when the sexual situation is transported into the moral realm: male sexual desire becomes a threat to "honor," while the female object of this desire becomes its cause and thus a force whose purpose is the corruption of this honor. In the American detective novel, the conflict between male and female has always been fought in the sexual arena. The unstated premise of the American detective novel is that the male needs the female for "sexual purposes" and that the female plays on this need to fulfill her own and largely nonsexual needs—for security, status, wealth, etc. Thus the ritualistic tempting of the detective with sexual favors, the vacillation of the detective between his attraction for and wariness of the women he encounters, and the preponderance of sexually attractive women who are exposed as the source of evil.

The American detective novel has always been obsessed with sex. It has also always linked sex with evil, violence, and death. Nowhere is this link more luridly graphic than on the covers of those thousands of American detective novels published in paperback over the last half century. Quasipornographic, these covers display the real subjects of the fictions they advertise: breasts and bullets, décolletage and death, desire and destruction. As Geoffrey O'Brien has said of these covers, "no trace of subtlety was permitted to cloud the violent and erotic visions that were their essence."[34] The point, of course, is not that hack writers and paperback publishers allowed the form to degenerate into a sexual sickness—although they certainly did that; it is, rather, that the only difference between the work of hacks and of "good" writers in the form is the difference in the intelligence and sophistication of their treatment of this central theme. The theme itself remains constant, as it does in much American fiction.

If the American detective novel is demonstrably American, it is also demonstrably a novel. As a genre, of course, the novel subsumes so many diverse types of fiction that anyone with a modicum of critical sense hesitates to make qualitative distinctions among them. But certainly there is a difference between what Conan Doyle and Dashiell Hammett were doing. Ross Macdonald, in fact, once nicely suggested that difference when he discriminated between the "English story of scientific detection à la Sherlock Holmes" and the detective novel that is "a form of the novel proper, subject like its other forms to the endless new developments which the word 'novel' suggests."[35]

The American detective novel, then, is characterized by its particular plot of detection and by its Americanness. As the formal detective story, with its emphasis on the preservation of social class structure, tends toward comic patterns of resolution, the hardboiled story concerns itself with the fate of the individual and is often oriented toward the tragic. Ideologically, it is an instrument not of social melioration but of social criticism—criticizing both the particular society it observes and the concept of society in general.

These characteristics notwithstanding, the American detective novel is also a remarkably flexible genre, allowing seemingly endless variations and innovations. As it developed, the American detective novel has continually adapted to the conditions of American life. Initially, for example, it took as its setting the city. In the work of Hammett and Chandler the urban environment is as crucial as it is in the novels of writers as different as Saul Bellow and Norman Mailer. But this has led some commentators to the notion that the form is restricted to this milieu. This despite the fact that Ross Macdonald quickly left the mean streets of the city for the winding drives of suburbia, and that American detective novels have had settings as diverse as the range/ranch/small-town Montana of James Crumley and the sand-and-swamp

Florida of John D. MacDonald. Nor must the detective be necessarily seedy, cynical, and alcoholic. Stephen Greenleaf Josh Tanner is a former attorney who makes a good living, works diligently, and drinks sparingly. And while another *Peanuts* cartoon has Lucy the critic insisting to Snoopy that he can't set a detective novel in Minneapolis, excellent novels well within the tradition have been set in Denver, Salt Lake City, Omaha, Seattle, and Indianapolis.

What critics like Lucy insist upon as conventional requirements of the American detective novel are largely superficialities, most of them informed by nostalgia. The conviction that the detective novel must develop the "urban wasteland" theme, for example, is similar to the belief that only Humphrey Bogart could portray Philip Marlowe on film. (The best portrayal of Marlowe, actually, is Robert Mitchum's in *Farewell, My Lovely*.) What these critics want is not generic but "formula" fiction. They can find it, of course, on any paperback rack in any airport or supermarket. They will not find it in the work of Ross Macdonald or those writers whom he so clearly influenced.

The distinction between the generic and the formulaic in detective fiction is crucial to any understanding of Ross Macdonald's art. Macdonald himself regularly discussed his work in terms of the genre, and his Lew Archer novels cannot be properly appreciated outside it. That tradition quite literally makes them what they are. Macdonald in his best work did not "transcend" the genre but rather developed some of its possibilities. That these possibilities were, and are, manifold is precisely what Hammett, Chandler, and Macdonald discovered and what remains unrecognized by those critics who would talk about formulas. The genre that these writers developed consists not of a formula but of a collection of motifs, ideas, situations, and patterns that novelists are free to use according to their purposes. If, as Gilbert Sorrentino says, the form is a "quite rigid and artificial structure,"[36] this rigidity and artificiality are relative. The picaresque novel, the bildungsroman, and the novel of manners are equally rigid and artificial, taking as their subjects specific aspects of human existence and developing these subjects in specific ways, to the exclusion of other human and aesthetic considerations.

Beyond that, however, the fictional possibilities inherent in the genre are unlimited. Most of the so-called conventions of the form are not formal requirements but simply stereotypes employed by hacks. Similar stereotypes dominated the early stories in the genre, until Hammett in effect defined the form in *The Maltese Falcon* by bringing to it a central theme and a pattern of purposeful, Aristotelian action. Hacks immediately transformed these features, as well as elements of setting, characterization, and ideology specific to that novel, into "conventions" that continued in popular versions of the genre until Raymond Chandler published *The Big Sleep.* So powerfully did Chandler imagine his detective that Marlowe then became the object of epigonic imitation, and his idosyncrasies and socioeconomic situation became "requirements" to unimaginative writers and careless critics. So it remained until Ross Macdonald developed a new set of attitudes, concerns, and techniques, and did this so well that "he is widely considered to have completed what Dashiell Hammett and Raymond Chandler began."[37]

Macdonald's Lew Archer novels did not do that, of course. The genre is alive and well, and many good writers are doing good and valuable things in it. If the form has not advanced notably in the last few years, it is not because it is "exhausted" or "no longer relevant" or "incapable of saying true things about life." It simply awaits another major figure—another Hammett, Chandler, or Macdonald—to discover more of its potential. Meanwhile, those who would reduce the form to a formula continue to insist that the American detective novel remain in the fictional world into which it was born.

Popular Fiction and Literature

While it finds its progenitors in major American fiction, the hardboiled detective novel was born and raised in popular culture, especially in the pulps of the 1920s and 1930s. The editors of *The Poetics of Murder* suggest that the fiction under consideration is "popular" because it enjoys a wide and continuing readership.[38] This is perhaps a partial definition of the term, but literary critics more often have in mind not the extent of readership but the authorial strategy of gaining that readership. What makes a work "popular" rather than "serious" is a clear intent to offer the reader confirmation of his "popular" biases, views, or ideologies.

As Michael Holquist has observed, popular literature gives its readers "not pain but bromides, not deep questions but easy answers"; it provides them with a "pattern of reassurance."[39] Popular literature is not escapist because it encourages the reader to flee life into unreality but because it depicts life in such a way as to resolve the real concerns of the reader. It is designed to palliate his problems, to applaud his holding specific views on the nature of human existence and society, to at once appeal to and reinforce his prejudices. Popular fiction is directed at a specific audience, produced by hacks following formulas purveyed by writers magazines, packaged in gaudy paperback covers, and dispensed in supermarkets and convenience stores. As products of our throwaway culture, popular books are read once and trashed.

This is not to argue that popular detective fiction must always be unsophisticated in technique or that its readers are 'intellectually disadvantaged,' as the current euphemism has it. Edmund Wilson and others have argued that most detective novels do not seriously engage the adult mind either morally or aesthetically,[40] but neither writers nor readers of detective fiction are necessarily cretinous. Many commentators have noted that intellectuals both read and write detective novels—in the hardboiled as well as the formal tradition. But the reasons they do so are as different as the forms.

The formal detective novel provides a test of mental agility, a puzzle to be solved. More subtly, however, it also argues for a view of life and society congenial to those who pride themselves on their rational abilities. As David Grossvogel observes in an essay on Agatha Christie, the formal detective novel posits a stable and rational society, then disturbs it by introducing evil in the form of a puzzling crime; in the action of the story, the detective—an amateur or a professional, a private citizen or an official social representative—logically fits together the pieces of the puzzle and solves the crime; thus, the fictional society regains its stability at the same time that the reader is assured that what he takes to be his own rational society is able to defend him against evil, that his society in fact contains within its structure the mechanism to defeat all evil. In the formal detective novel, rational acuity and ingenuity both explain the existence of evil and thwart its impulses in a basically good and secure society. Rationality triumphs in a rational world.[41]

Intellectuals also read hardboiled novels, but they read fewer of them. Mostly they read Hammett, Chandler, and Macdonald, or they read others looking for the qualities they find in these writers. In these novels they find a puzzle or mystery, the solution to which provides some pleasure. The widespread critical assumption that the hardboiled detective novel ignores the detection element[42] is not demonstrable in much of the fiction. What is demonstrable is that the Aristotelian nature of the plot subordinates detection to moral and aesthetic objectives. Thus, these books can be read not as puzzles but as novels. And in these novels readers find a worldview antithetical to that of the formal detective story.

The popular hardboiled detective novel portrays society as essentially corrupt. Crime is the result of irrational forces or elemental human vices, sometimes even the inevitable effect of the societal effort itself, and a specific manifestation of a general social and moral malaise. The detective, usually a "private" investigator licensed (that is, at once tolerated and partially controlled) by his society, solves the crime, often despite the efforts of the society against which he must struggle, a society that would dissuade him with sex, money, or violence from his exposure of its fundamental corruption and from his pursuit of the justice it will not or cannot effect. The reader derives pleasure from the depiction of an unjust society that rewards evil rather than good and so confirms his sense of life's injustice; from the fictional assertion that his own unsettling impulses are common to humanity; and from the argument that the individual can, through physical strength and courage tempered by a private code of honor, redress the wrongs done or condoned by that society. Violence triumphs in a violent world.

As Holquist suggests, each form of popular literature—be it either type of detective novel, mysteries, thrillers, spy fiction, science fiction, Gothic romances, or what even in this postfeminist period can be described only as "women's novels"—offers to its readers a "particular pattern of reassurance." But this lowbrow strategy is not inherent in the forms of the fiction. These simply serve as effective media for dissemination throughout the culture of the platitudes from which so many of its members take comfort. It is not the forms that are "popular" but the simplistic message that hacks transmit through them.

That this is the case is illustrated by the endings of two of the most widely read American detective novels, Dashiell Hammett's *The Maltese Falcon* and Mickey Spillane's *I, the Jury*. Each novel ends with the detective rejecting the woman to whom he is attracted, but the manner, terms, and thematic implications of the rejection differ radically. Cawelti has incisively assessed the conclusion of Spillane's novel, where the detective confronts the murderer who is also the woman he desires. Charlotte Manning, the beautiful psychiatrist, strips before Mike Hammer and "as she offers her naked charms to him, he shoots her. Thus possession and destruction reach a simultaneous climax. Doubtless, it is Spillane's ability to create images that embody these symbolic tensions and resolutions in the most simplified fashion that accounts for his extraordinary popularity."[43] In this astonishing scene, Spillane has Mike Hammer, the surrogate for and champion of the novel's typical male reader, both confirm and avenge the supposed wrongs done him by women, the intellectual, and the wealthy. At the same time he validates the quasisadistic and machismo-laden code by which he and his readers would live: "No, Charlotte, I'm the jury now, and the judge, and I have a promise to keep. Beautiful as you are, as much as I almost loved you, I sentence you to death."[44]

How different the ending of *The Maltese Falcon,* where Sam Spade rejects Brigid O'Shaughnessy, the murderer of his partner. Resisting her entreaties and appeals to love, he turns her over to the police because that's his business, and in his world there is nothing else. Miss Wonderly has been exposed as the corrupt Brigid, the Maltese Falcon has been revealed as a worthless lump of lead, and "to gamble on Brigid O'Shaughnessy is like gambling that love exists, or that there is, somewhere, a genuine Falcon."[45] So much for the "easy reassurances" of the American detective novel.

I stress this point only because of the power with which the assumptions about popular fiction shape discussions of all detective novels, even those clearly of an authorial intent and ultimate effect irreconcilable with the "popular strategy." The result of these assumptions is that evaluations of detective novels as novels are few and apologetic, partly, as Frank Kermode has noted, because "they are thought by some to be unworthy of it."[46] And certainly many, perhaps most, of these works do not lend themselves to literary analysis. Thus, for some critics all detective novels "have come to be seen as contemporary folktales, cultural documents par excellence, and prime illustrations of mental and social processes."[47] Or they serve as structures ideal for the working out of new theories of narratology. Meanwhile, works that through their moral and aesthetic qualities ask to be treated as "serious" or "art" or "literature" are considered, if indeed they are considered at all, as presumptuous.

The prevailing view of detective fiction holds that the form itself dooms to failure any attempt to do serious things in it. One critic who defends this view is Geoffrey Hartman. He too confuses genres, but he states clearly the "literary" objection to detective fiction: "Few detective novels want the reader to exert his intelligence fully, to find gaps in the plot or the reasoning, to worry about the moral question of fixing the blame. They are exorcism stories with happy endings that could be classified with comedy because they settle the unsettling."[48] The qualifying "few" suggests that Hartman would exempt some detective novels from his censure, but despite the many excellences he finds in the *The Underground Man,* he relegates it with those that "settle the unsettling." To do so he must misread the novel, the ending of which is more unsettling than he would have it. His assessment accurately describes much of the work in the genre, but it does not reflect the literary qualities of *The Maltese Falcon, Farewell, My Lovely, The Long Goodbye,* or several novels by Ross Macdonald—all of which do not presume to be "serious" or "art" or "literature" but are in fact these things.

Art, Literature, and Value

What is presumptuous, of course, is the way we use these terms. The phrase "serious novel" means, if it actually means anything, that the novel compels us to read it with moral and aesthetic seriousness. But no fictional form carries with it a mechanism to prompt serious reading. A work of fiction is serious only to the extent that it requires us to treat it seriously.[49] And all fiction is "art"—the word identifies the product of a type of human activity. Fiction can vary in technical sophistication, moral significance, and emotional effect, but it is all by definition literary art, as someone like Mickey Spillane is a literary artist—if not a very good one.

But if all fiction is art, it is not all "literature"—not, at least, as the term is used in academic and critical discussions. In such discussions we apply "literature" as an honorific, indicating superior achievement. Recent literary theory has demonstrated, however, that we do so on the basis of attitudes that we can't really support. As Terry Eagleton has shown, all attempts to define the essence of literature, to isolate the "literary," have failed; they must fail, for "'literature' and 'weed' are *functional* rather than *ontological* terms."[50] The word says nothing about the essence of a particular work; it describes only the value we place on that work. Literature is simply writing valued by the culture.

By and large, we haven't valued detective novels much, as we indicate by both our critical neglect and the kind of critical attention we pay them—as documents of sociological import, as quaint artifacts dredged from the slough of popular culture. I am arguing that some hardboiled detective novels demand consideration as literature, as "valued writing." Before that can happen, of course, we must agree on a criteria of value. From his Marxist position, Eagleton argues that our valuing of certain works is a matter of ideology.[51] Still, insofar as the novel is concerned, there is a general consensus about value. Three critics of decidedly different orientation, all of whom happen to be writing about detective novels, express in their own terms the same basic requirement. Fredric Jameson, another Marxist critic, talks about "the registering apparatus of great literature" that invariably effects "some Joycean epiphany."[52] Geoffrey Hartman gives the same notion a different emphasis, arguing that the detective novelist should "show us more about life—that is, about the way people die while living. What is uncovered is not death but death-in-life."[53] But Sheldon Sacks, addressing Ross Macdonald's work, presents this idea most effectively when he describes the Lew Archer novels as "significantly moving human actions" in which the reader follows "Lew Archer as he pursues with success solutions to labyrinthine riddles of human violence and with inevitable failure pursues mysteries of human guilt and hate and love."[54]

If we cannot define literature, we can measure its effect. We can also delin-

eate the artistic methods that create that effect. This is the task of the following pages—to show which of Macdonald's novels are "significantly moving
human actions" and to identify the art that makes them so. To do either of
these things, of course, we must assess them in their own terms—as American detective novels.

Chapter Three
Searching for Lew Archer

It has been suggested that Ross Macdonald's first four novels "look to the more accomplished work which followed."[1] This is both accurate and charitable. These early works establish some of the themes that Macdonald was to develop more skillfully later in his career, and they demonstrate specific aspects of craft that were to become central to his mature art. They are not, however, very good. Had there been no Archer novels, none of Macdonald's first four attempts at fiction would justify critical consideration, and none is of interest other than to illustrate how far Macdonald managed to surpass his early efforts.

The two espionage novels, *The Dark Tunnel* and *Trouble Follows Me*, reveal their author's skill with language, as well as his debt to writers like Stephen Crane, Dashiell Hammett, and Raymond Chandler and to the cinema. The third novel, *Blue City*, is thoroughly within the tradition Hammett epitomized with his Continental Op stories. And *The Three Roads*, the most ambitious of the books published under Macdonald's real name, treats many of the psychosexual themes that lurk beneath the surface of the later novels. The first four novels show Macdonald writing some fine sentences and solid scenes, sometimes finding thematically revealing images, and developing a surer sense of the relations among action, character, and theme. The first three are imitative, but that in itself is not the problem; the problem, which they share with the fourth, lies in their narrative perspective. In these books Macdonald experiments with narrators, searching for the character or method that will allow the exercise of his many natural gifts and at the same time provide a clear and steady focus on his material. He finds it, of course, in private detective Lew Archer, the narrator of the fifth novel, *The Moving Target*.

Of Nazis, Negroes, and Narrators

The Dark Tunnel (1944) seems the work of a writer whose goal was to be published. Its pandering to popular notions of Nazi decadence and homosexual villainy ensured a receptive wartime audience, as did its sentimental

ending. These features perhaps distracted attention from the story, which
hinges on coincidences of colossal proportions, from a confused pattern of
sexual imagery, and from the narrator-hero, whose character shifts according
to the dictates of the action and the exegetical impulses of the author.

As the novel opens, Assistant Professor Robert Branch, after being turned
down by the military because of poor eyesight, returns from Detroit to Midwestern University and learns two things: that "there's been a leakage of information from the War Board to Nazi agents"[2] and that Ruth Esch, of
whom Branch became enamored while in Germany six years before, will
soon arrive to take a position in the German department. Branch muses,
"Now coincidence had reached across the ocean and she was coming to
Arbana" (16). Coincidence, it turns out, has done considerably more than
that. An actress when Branch knew her, Ruth had also been a student of Professor Herman Schneider, formerly "the greatest Shakespearian scholar in
Germany" (16), now teaching at Midwestern University. Professor Schneider
is also the primary suspect in the espionage plot and the father of Peter
Schneider, arch villain, Nazi agent, and homosexual, whose lover is Carl
Esch, the brother of Ruth and the Nazi officer who struck Branch with his
swagger stick and injured his eye. Everything in the novel depends on that in-
jured eye, for after having his eyeglasses smashed in a duel of phallic sabers
with Peter Schneider, Branch sees Peter kissing Ruth, who is not supposed to
have arrived. Of course it is not Ruth whom Peter is kissing but her brother
Carl in drag, but because of his injured eye Branch can't make the distinction.
(What his other, good eye is doing at the time our hero doesn't mention.)
Soon bodies appear, Branch is suspected of murder, a chase ensues, and
Branch solves the mystery, exposes the espionage ring, and subdues Peter
Schneider, after which, "At the end of the tunnel Ruth was waiting with her
hair bright as sunlight and no sword in her hand" (247).

This from a novelist who would extol the virtues of meaningful action and
see plot "as a vehicle of meaning [that] should be as complex as contemporary life, but balanced enough to say true things about it" (*SP*, 120). Still, *The
Dark Tunnel* has some good things in it. Many of the scenes are vivid, and the
supporting characters are well drawn; the portrait of the besieged Professor
Herman Schneider is, in fact, excellent. The chase sequence, of the John
Buchan and *The Thirty-nine Steps* variety, has enough energy, tension, and
incidents to distract attention from its essential implausibility, and a "locked
room" mystery is cleverly handled. The texture of the novel is often rich, and
many of the images are fresh or powerful. Some of these are merely decora-
tive—"The juke box at the back of the room looked like a French chateau
that had swallowed a rainbow" (8); others express a naturalistic vision like

that of Stephen Crane, whose prose Macdonald's sometimes resembles: "In the nightmare sequence of events that had seemed to grow out of each other, meaninglessly and malignantly, like cancer cells, I saw the push of giant uncontrollable forces on weak men, the waste of breakable wills and stout fragile bodies fractured in the clash of continents" (244).

The real problem with the novel, however, is Robert Branch. As both character and narrator, Branch confuses rather than clarifies. Macdonald would have his protagonist a universal and democratic hero, a man equally at home in academe and alleyways, but the yoking of antithetical characteristics into a two-fisted scholar strains credulity. That the combination never solidifies is evidenced by Branch's narrative voice; in it are suggestions of the Continental Op on the one hand and Philip Marlowe on the other, of Crane's imagistic darkness and Hemingway's tough terseness. The humor is Chandlerian, Philip Marlowe's ironic rhythms infused with academic pretension: "Arbana is the Athens of the West and McKinley Hall is its Parthenon and I am Pericles" (12). Branch's literary allusions contribute little to the narrative, his party-line liberalism offers no real insight into the subjects upon which he is wont to pontificate, and his physical prowess comes into play because of actions at odds with his professorial rationality. Confusions riddle the narration, as Branch regularly puts his peril on hold to interject observations that the author seems to find of more interest than the fate of his hero.

In retrospect, of course, we can see what Macdonald wished to do with Branch and the novel he narrates. We can also see how he fails. The twin demands he places on his narrator-hero tug Branch first one way, then another, so that he functions well in neither role. The artistic problem that *The Dark Tunnel* reveals—the inability to create a coherent and authoritative narrative consciousness—Macdonald struggled to solve in his next three novels as well.

Trouble Follows Me (1946) is a small step toward the narrator Macdonald was to discover in Lew Archer. Naval Ensign Sam Drake is a more probable version of Robert Branch. Another educated tough guy—"I'm an intellectual among roughnecks and a roughneck among intellectuals"[3]—Drake was a newspaperman before the war, and while quick with an allusion and a compulsive maxim-maker, he is less sententious and physically adept than Branch. Still, he too acts from the dictates of the plot rather than from his character; a quarter of the way through the book he realizes that he has neither the skill nor the experience to deal with the case and should leave its solution to the FBI, then for no apparent motive continues to pursue it.

The plot of this novel is stronger, but Macdonald still resorts to coincidences to keep it going. More important, the impact of the action is enfeebled by a conclusion that shows the author again playing to the expectations of his popular audience. Along with the espionage plot, the novel develops the romantic relationship of Drake and Mary Thompson, friend and coworker of the first murder victim. At the novel's end, Mary is exposed as a spy and a murderer, and Sam Drake "sees" her for the first time: "I saw that like all true criminals she was abnormal. Part of her sensibility was missing and part of her mind was blank. She could not see herself as evil or depraved. Her ego stood between her and the rest of the world like a distorting lens" (192). What is being distorted here is the narrative, for the reader, who has lived with Mary for nearly two hundred pages, cannot see her as evil or depraved either. Nary a hint or gesture has suggested that she is perhaps not the woman she seems, so the reversal strikes us as extrinsic to the action, reversal for reversal's sake. Macdonald uses the ending of *The Maltese Falcon* without the pattern of revelatory action that gave it power and meaning.

Trouble Follows Me is more ambitious than Macdonald's first spy novel, aspiring both to suspense and seriousness. Macdonald handles its serious subject, race relations, better than he did the Nazi evil at the heart of the first book. Here the subject arises from the action and is, for the most part, presented dramatically. Although the post-1960s sensibility may find Macdonald's treatment of racism idealistic, his effort is honest and avoids stereotyped black characters if not conventional liberal aperçus on the problem.

Trouble Follows Me is more coherent than *The Dark Tunnel*, the atmosphere less grimly naturalistic, the prose more fluid and less imitative, the discourse less pretentious. Again, minor characters are well drawn and many of the scenes are vivid. The problems of Macdonald's second novel, however, result from the same cause as those of his first. As both hero and narrator, Sam Drake demands at once our emotional involvement with his predicament and our acceptance of his judgments about the nature and significance of the other characters and the action. Since it is precisely these judgments that create Drake's predicament, the reader cannot simultaneously respond both ways; he can only watch Drake vacillate between his roles as hero and as commentator on the quality of his own heroism. Because of the protagonist's bifurcation, the action can neither arise from nor reveal his character and must be dictated by the author. While getting a firmer grip on the problem that plagued his art, Macdonald was far from solving it.

An Angry Rapture

Macdonald wrote both *Blue City* and *The Three Roads* in the same ten months, "in a kind of angry rapture" (*SP,* 26). The two novels reflect, even perhaps revel in that anger. Whatever rapture might have been involved, however, seems to have been restricted to the consciousness of their author, for both works are dark, grim, and troubled, ultimately not so much rapturous as bewildering. In *Blue City* Macdonald tried to continue the hardboiled tradition exemplified by Hammett's *Red Harvest,* examining urban corruption and the violence to which it inevitably gives rise, while in *The Three Roads* he welded Freudian concepts and structures into a psychodrama of sex and murder that borrows heavily from Hitchcockian film noir. While they share the exile-and-return theme and some stylistic qualities, the two novels differ so radically in form, ambience, and attitude that their having been written by the same man at the same time is little short of astonishing. Viewed together, they suggest why Macdonald found it impossible to follow them with a "serious" novel based on his childhood.

Blue City (1947) is the angriest book Macdonald ever wrote, and the most violent. The violence arises from the anger of the narrator hero John Weather; because that anger is neither explained nor developed, however, the violence is largely gratuitous. The anger of John Weather, in fact, comes not from the character but from the author. Macdonald later admitted this: "it was about a town where I had suffered, and several of the characters were based on people I hated."[4] An obvious projection of adolescent male fantasy, John Weather at twenty-two weighs "a hundred and eighty stripped and was almost as fast as a welterweight,"[5] fears neither fists nor guns, reacts to beatings with wisecracks, and brings a prostitute to orgasm and true love. At the same time he is a "man who knows ideas" (38), and he is as fast with a lecture on the socioeconomic ills of the age as he is with his fists. Weather is, finally, impossible to take seriously, as is the novel he narrates. One reviewer described *Blue City* as "very, very tough, and a little silly too,"[6] and so it is.

Nevertheless, in *Blue City* Macdonald does some new and some good things. He creates a society and delineates some of the economic and emotional links among its various levels. His portrait of the underside of the city, for all John Weather's grim anger and tedious moralizing, is sharply etched and recognizably real. Minor characters are again well drawn, descriptions fix the physical and moral decay of urban blight in strong images, and the prose often crackles with energy. The action of the novel, which follows Weather's attempt to identify the murderer of his father and to begin the cleanup of a city rotting with civic venality and social and sexual corruption, is largely of a piece, more integrated with character and theme than in the previous books, and unmarred by serious coincidence. Like its predecessors, *Blue City* evidences both compositional problems and authorial promise.

Those problems are even more serious and that promise less near fulfillment in *The Three Roads* (1948). An ambitious work, it perhaps seems a more egregious failure than it really is, but it succeeds only in demonstrating the seriousness of the technical problems Macdonald had been unable to overcome and his inability to transform into realized art material about which he felt strongly. An attempt to reach a more sophisticated audience, *The Three Roads* aspires to intellectual substance and artistic accomplishment. What it achieves is confusion and incoherence. Macdonald wrote to one of his critics that he was forced by his editors to excise a hundred pages from the novel "for the market,"[7] which may account for its disjointed structure; if the missing pages contain the same treatment of the same material as those that remain, however,we would not wish them back on any account.

Macdonald's only novel to use an omniscient narrator, *The Three Roads* tells the story of Naval Lieutenant Bret Taylor's "rebirth" after nine months in the psychiatric ward of a Naval hospital, where he was placed for treatment of the amnesia that began when he discovered his murdered wife. As his recovery begins, Taylor gradually remembers that his wife was killed, and he learns that the crime has never been solved; under the twin impulses of the need to know the truth of his past and the desire to effect justice, he sets out to discover the identity of the murderer. What he finds, like Oedipus, is himself.

The Oedipus story, in both its Sophoclean and Freudian versions, informs the action of the novel and explains the characters. In fact, a brace of psychiatrists, as well as Taylor and his girlfriend Paula West, couch in Freudian terms explanations of almost everything. Yet the novel is not "about" psychological theory. The subject of *The Three Roads* is love, specifically sexual love. Taylor, like Oedipus, has been exiled from love by what he thinks was the death of his mother, a psychic trauma exacerbated by the misogynistic proclamations of his emotionally and sexually enervated father (allusions to D. H. Lawrence invoke *Lady Chatterly's Lover* as a paradigm). Also like Oedipus, Taylor has been crippled through this exile, suffering a psychosexual lameness. A virgin at thirty, Taylor falls in love with Paula West while on leave from the Navy, but he makes no attempt to consummate that love. On another leave, after a spat with Paula, he gets drunk, picks up a girl in a bar and sleeps with her, and in a fit of guilt marries her the following day. On yet another leave he finds his wife in an adulterous tryst, and he kills her before swooning into unconsciousness and amnesia. All this we learn and Taylor remembers as he tracks his wife's killer and slowly recovers the past. We and Taylor also learn that his mother is not dead, that she had abandoned her family after her four-year-old son discovered her in bed with her lover; the son, Bret, had attacked his mother, and his father's subsequent assertion that she was dead convinced him that he had killed her.

We grant the author his subject, be it primal scene psychodrama or sexual and emotional dysfunctioning. The question is what he can do with it, and Macdonald does some curious things in *The Three Roads*. Just how curious we see in the images that pervade the novel. Paula West, for example, stumbles against Taylor "and his muscles tightened in her hand and became as hard as wood. It gave her a queer feeling, and a rather frightening one, which her fancy translated into an image of the body beneath the blue uniform, a body carved by exertion, pared lean by the wind, polished by the sun, with blankness like a fig leaf guarding her mind from the bronzed loins."[8] In the next paragraph she perceives the crashing of the surf onto rocks as being "like the mating of horses" (29). One of the minor characters watches his naked girlfriend walk toward him. "Her navel and two nipples made a cartoon of another face, a long and mournful one" (91). As for Bret Taylor, responding to his wife's body he feels that "the sweep of her hips was terrifying, and the blandness of her belly and thighs, and the panther blackness of her hair" (61); yet he later suspects that "he was only one in a long series of lovers that did not end with him, a second-class private in the nocturnal army that had bivouacked on her young *mons*" (146). Then there are passages like this: "Swayed heavily by the alcoholic pulse that was rising and falling in his brain, his imagination saw with hysteric clarity the pipes of sewage that branched like infected veins through all the streets of all the cities, the beast with two backs crying its rut in a thousand undomesticated bedrooms, the insatiable appetite of female loins and the brutal meat that fed those blind adulterous mouths" (103).

This sort of "hysteric clarity" is perhaps justified in Bret Taylor's consciousness; unfortunately, it infects all the characters. Beyond that, while Taylor's pathology is manifestly conscious to both character and author, that of Paula West appears not to be. At the end of the first chapter, she is worried: "She had him in her grasp for a moment, and then he had slipped away again, to a place where she did not dare to follow" (8). In the same conversation she can both chastise Taylor's wife for viewing him as "an acquisition" (17) and lament that Taylor "belonged to another woman" (15). And try as they might, neither she nor her creator can explain her obsessive need to possess and control a man of whom she feels "there was something pathetically arid about his kiss, as if the tropical sun had evaporated his vital juices" (35). On the one hand we are told, "In the two and a half years since she had met Bret Taylor there had been stirrings in the heart of her body as heavy and ultimate as seismic movements. She had to admit that she was beginning to feel as female as hell, as female as any D. H. Lawrence *Fraulein"* (22); while on the other hand, "the physical inadequacy of his kiss didn't matter" (35).

It is difficult to determine what to make of all this. Nor is it clear how we are to take the conclusion of the novel. When Taylor discovers that he murdered his wife, he does not turn himself in because of his desire to protect Paula, who has lied to the police—this after the action of the novel has been motivated by his desire for justice. And what are we to make of this Oedipus figure docilely being led offstage by Paula, not to exile but to bed? The action and attitudes of the novel render the conclusion so problematical that one critic can assert that it "is one of Macdonald's most positive—a man and a woman in love, fully aware of the collective past and their own individual pasts and limitations, walk arm and arm up the stairs to bed."9

Less difficult to perceive is that our uncertainty results from Macdonald's own, and that the authorial confusion derives as much from the narrative perspective as anything else. The third-person narrator allows Macdonald to present different views of the subject, but by dipping in and out of various consciousnesses he fails to get the objectifying distance he needs to clarify the implications of that action. In fact, the omniscience of the narrator reduces the distance, immersing narrator in character and often blurring the distinction between the two. If the action is confused as the result of the cutting required by Knopf, the novel as a whole is confused by the author's inability to distinguish and maintain distance between character and narrator. The consequence is fictional disaster.

The New-Type Detective

That Macdonald's publishers found his fifth novel a departure from his previous work is not surprising. That they found it inferior is astonishing. *The Moving Target* (1949) is so much better than anything Macdonald had done before that it constitutes a kind of quantum leap to a higher level of artistic performance. And what powered this leap was his conception and creation of the private detective and narrator Lew Archer.

"I'm the new-type detective,"10 Archer announces early in the novel, and so he is, although in ways not immediately apparent. At first glance, he seems a thoroughly and imitatively Marlovian figure, another version of the tough private eye whose surface cynicism masks a moral and somewhat sentimental nature, one more lone and slightly melancholy male so estranged from society that he can find meaning for his life only in the lives of others. Lew Archer, like Chandler's Philip Marlowe, is all of these. He is also a man of little formal education but keen intelligence and broad experience, a man whose knowledge of psychological, social, and cultural matters, as well as of life of the streets, is sufficient that we can trust his judgments, and who expresses these judgments in an American prose that fuses vernacular rhythms and often striking images.

But even in his initial appearance Lew Archer reveals a nature more complex than Marlowe's or those of the private eyes created by Chandler's many pulp-writing epigones. His isolation, for example, has a cause—the destruction of his marriage, for which he suffers not only loneliness but also guilt. That guilt is exacerbated by his job and some of the methods he must use in doing it. In the first novel he narrates, for example, Archer feigns sexual interest in and encourages the intoxication of a woman from whom he needs information. He silently assesses himself: "I was a good Joe after all. Consorter with roughnecks, tarts, hard cases and easy marks; private eye at the keyhole of illicit bedrooms; informer to jealousy, rat behind the walls, hired gun to anybody with fifty dollars a day; but a good Joe after all" (55). Later he moves from a bar stool "with gigolo alacrity" (56), and he responds to the woman's declarations that he's "nice" first with the observation that "my skin was thin enough to feel the irony" (56) and later with another cynical self-criticism: "Yeah, I said to myself, a clean-cut American type. Always willing to lend a hand to help a lady fall flat on her face in the gutter" (46). The next day he describes to another character his "feeding alcohol to an alcoholic," and sums up his feeling about it and himself: "The judge suspended sentence, but he gave me a tongue-lashing" (111). A man of neither impenetrable probity nor morbid self-flagellation, Archer looks on himself as he looks on the characters whose stories he tells, for he knows that he is one of them.

Knowing himself as such, Archer also knows that he is capable of the same evil that they so often enact, for "evil isn't so simple. Everybody has it in him, and whether it comes out in his actions depends on a number of things. Environment, opportunity, economic pressure, a piece of bad luck, a wrong friend" (109). This view contrasts sharply with that of Sam Spade or the Continental Op, for whom everyone will do evil, or that of Marlowe, who tends to see people in absolute terms. It also makes his job different. "But most of my work is watching people, and judging them" (110). And while he can mock himself in this activity—"I'm developing into quite a moralist in early middle age" (110)—his judgments are informed by understanding and a not a little sympathy.

Lew Archer as a character does not account for the superiority of *The Moving Target*, however; it is his function as narrator that gives the novel its distinction. Here Macdonald separates his narrator and hero. Archer acts, and we attend closely to his actions, but he is more important as a catalyst for the actions of the other characters, and it is these characters and their actions that hold our attention. Archer tells the story, but it is not his story. Nor does he alone bear the burden of our emotional involvement. That is spread among the other characters. By shifting attention away from his narrator, Macdonald established the basis of the intricate narrative art that he was to perfect in later books.

Art from the Outside

The essence of this art lies in precisely what Macdonald always did best. In the earlier novels, he demonstrated a talent for creating minor or secondary characters. Because his focus was on the narrator-hero, he sketched these characters with an almost cinematic objectivity, from the outside, through individualizing gestures and telling speech patterns and revealing physical or sartorial detail; after a snatch of dialogue or a brief scene, they stood clearly and fully formed before us. Now, with Archer as narrator but not subject, Macdonald's focus is on the other characters, but it is still objective, so they can be revealed only through action, dialogue, and images filtered through Archer's consciousness.

The art of *The Moving Target,* and of the novels that follow it, is dramatic rather than expository. It precludes most introspective inquiries into emotions, allows no lengthy musing on the implications of situation and action; it eliminates the self-examination and analysis that frequently bogged down the action and confused the themes of the earlier novels. While Archer still has much to say about the people he meets and the society they constitute— and about himself—the impulse toward explanation is restrained. Much of the novel reads, in fact, like a narrated film script; we believe of and feel for the characters as we do because of how they appear to us rather than because the narrator tells us what to believe and feel. Macdonald recognized this, once observing that "*The Moving Target* in particular is a story clearly aspiring to be a movie" (*SP,* 36).

The artistic implications of this new narrative perspective are profound, for the techniques of character and thematic development it requires lend themselves perfectly to detective fiction. In effect, as an Archer novel opens, there are no obviously central characters. All characters are observed from the outside, and neither Lew Archer nor the reader knows which will play the leading role in the action. Early in the novel Archer evaluates and judges all the characters on an equal basis; as the action proceeds, he circles back to those who seem most involved in or implicated by that action; in different settings and circumstances, characters manifest different qualities, so that through sharp observation and subtle questioning Archer exposes different aspects of character, significance of action, and ramifications of theme; gradually the centrality of some characters becomes apparent, the circle narrows, and finally Archer discovers the truth about the characters, the action, the crimes, and the case.

Placing Lew Archer on the emotional periphery of the novel offered Macdonald additional artistic opportunities, especially in his use of language, in the creation of contrapuntal structures, and in the elucidation of character and meaning. Because he did with these aspects of narrative art things different from—if not necessarily superior to—what Hammett and Chandler did, however, their artistic purpose has been misunderstood by some readers.

Lew Archer is a character in the novels he narrates. Because of his dual function, his language also has a dual function. As narrator, Archer is the perceiving consciousness of the novels; the story unfolds before his eyes, its patterns coalesce in his consciousness, and its meaning comes to us primarily in his language. The same language that describes setting and character and action, and expresses Archer's observations and ruminations, however, also characterizes Archer. Frequently, Archer's language is slightly at odds with its object, his descriptions larded with the distinctive qualities of his consciousness. This allows Macdonald to create some interesting if subtle effects.

Beyond that, while Archer is Macdonald's narrator, he is not necessarily his spokesman. Archer the narrator recounts events as Archer the character experienced them, but these events are organized by the author. As Macdonald wrote to one of his critics, the novels are "imagined actions seen in imagined retrospect,"[11] but while the action and retrospect are Lew Archer's, the imagination—the organization and structure—of both are Ross Macdonald's. Archer interprets events in terms of his own consciousness, with all his idiosyncratic attitudes, concerns, and problems. But as narrator he is a "deliberately narrowed version of the writing self." He sees what he sees, but he does not see what the author sees. As Daniel Barnes has pointed out, Archer is often "fallible";[12] his assessment of character is often initially incorrect, and sometimes it remains so. Frequently, Archer explains a situation one way, to his own satisfaction, while the novel as a whole provides a quite different explanation—the endings of *The Ivory Grin* and *The Underground Man* illustrate this distinction.

All this is to say that the relationship of narrator to author in Macdonald's novels is far more complex and problematic than it first appears, and that the novels are far more intricately devised than they might seem at first reading. The story that Archer tells is not always the story that Macdonald tells. Macdonald was aware that many readers did not perceive this and that many

critics failed to attend to its implications. As he once remarked, "there hasn't
been very imaginative understanding of the nature of first-person narration
in criticism."[13]

Placing Archer at the emotional edge of the story he narrates solved another of Macdonald's problems. In the early books he had attempted to follow Chandler's lead by allowing the central character to tell his own story.
This convention dominated the form at the time, and Chandler developed it
with particular effectiveness. The primary subject of his fiction was Philip
Marlowe, his emotions and sensibility and responses. Because of this, the
characters Marlowe dealt with tended toward the extreme, were grotesques
designed to effect the most immediate and intense response; their purpose
was less to engage the reader's sympathy than to provide Marlowe the opportunity to reveal elements of his personality. In the work of less imaginative
writers, of course, these grotesques degenerated into stereotypes. Macdonald,
however, chose not to make Archer the center of emotional concern; this required that the emotional burden of the novels fall on one or more of the
other characters, and this in turn required that these characters be human,
characters about whose fate we could be made to care. Usually, the Archer
novels center emotionally in one or two characters involved in the case, and
Archer functions as a sort of emotional guide, directing the reader's response
to these characters. His emotional involvement is not the focus of our concern
but rather the device by which we focus that concern on another character.

The narrative distancing of this technique has further aesthetic implications. Because character is revealed in part through the details of environment
and setting, these are especially important; they are clues leading toward the
truth of character rather than toward solution of the crime. This precludes description for its own sake. Image as well as action is "not just a decoration, it's
a carrier of meaning."[14] The rich texture of the narratives, about which so
many critics have commented, is not simply "fine writing" but an integral
part of the structure. Image functions much like character, taking on different shades of meaning as it recurs in different situations, finally becoming—
and this is especially true in the later novels—not image but symbol, "where
it is intended to have deep psychological and social meanings."[15]

It should be noted that the significance of these descriptions was one
Macdonald did not immediately appreciate. The early Archer novels do in
fact contain set pieces of fine writing. More than anything they indicate the
influence of Raymond Chandler, an influence Macdonald was not to escape
for several years. When he did come to make the American detective novel
the medium for expressing his own vision, the descriptive passages as well as

Archer's overt moral evaluations of character and society became less frequent and more relevant to the story he was telling.

The Moving Target freed Macdonald from the problems he had with other narrative perspectives. Paradoxically, he effected this liberation by accepting the severe limitations imposed by the external and objective view of Lew Archer. But with these restrictions came both the distance necessary for him to view his material clearly and the sharp and steady focus required to understand it. Thus the creation of a "new-type" detective and a new narrative focus also allowed him to begin the exploration of what was to become the central subject of his later fiction. While he was to write several more novels before he committed himself to this subject, Macdonald in his first Archer book laid out its central concerns.

Staking a Claim

The Moving Target involves Archer in a possible, then probable, and finally certain kidnapping. Ralph Sampson, an alcoholic Texas wildcatter who has moved his oil money and his family to Southern California, disappears after a flight from Santa Teresa to Burbank. Because Sampson is irresponsible with money when drunk, his wife wants him found. Albert Graves, the Sampsons's lawyer and Archer's former boss in the D.A.'s office, recommends Archer. The detective interviews the family—Sampson's paralytic second wife and former mistress Elaine, and his daughter, Miranda—and the help, primarily Sampson's pilot, Allan Taggert. Returning to Los Angeles to pick up Sampson's trail, Archer finds himself involved with assorted crackpots and low lifes—a buxom astrologer, her cold and criminal husband, and a hulking thug named Puddler; a jazz pianist in a B-joint; a scrawny hood and his ex-hooker wife; a self-styled cult priest. Gradually he connects these people with the Sampson family. A letter from Sampson arrives asking that money be made ready; a ransom note follows. The drop is made, and a body results. Archer makes more connections, links the characters, and finds Ralph Sampson dead. Finally he discovers the identity of Sampson's killer.

Most of this is nicely handled; the pace is swift, the characterization solid, the mood and suspense effectively modulated, the scenes sharp, and the action largely free of obvious authorial manipulation. The action reveals character, which reveals connections between characters and lends meaning to the action. Archer discovers the meaning of the action not, however, in the crank- and crook-infested sprawl of Los Angeles but in the Sampson household and the miasma of poisoned and poisoning love enshrouding it. As he traces the human links in a chain of crime, he also charts the moral deterioration and the inevitable dissolution of the Sampson family.

That the Sampson family is in serious trouble is clear from the beginning of the novel. Several characters observe that neither Ralph Sampson nor his wife has recovered from the death of Sampson's son, a navy flier killed in the war. Near the end of the novel, Elaine Sampson tells Archer that she was "widowed" by her stepson's death (238), and the loss of his son has intensified Sampson's drinking, his ruthlessness in business, and his involvement with spiritual hucksters. But the marriage has long been troubled.

The Sampsons married after Elaine had failed in several careers for which she had no talent. A woman of no concerns other than "greed and vanity" (22), whose "age was as hard to tell as the age of a figure carved from mahogany" (5) but who admits to being twenty years her husband's junior, she tells Archer: "I want my marriage to last. You see, I intend to outlive my husband" (6). Of Sampson she says, "A few drinks, and he wants to be a little boy again. He goes looking for a mother type or father type to blow his nose and dry away his tears and spank him when he's naughty. Do I sound cruel? I'm simply being objective" (8). That he might be with another woman concerns her only to the extent that "I'll want to know all about her because I couldn't afford to give away an advantage like that" (9). Sampson himself does not appear in the story until Archer finds his body in the penultimate chapter. In a prophetic photograph, however, Archer sees Sampson's inevitable end, and his own: "The smile that folded the puffed eyelids and created the sagging cheeks was fixed and forced. I'd seen such smiles in mortuaries on the false face of death. It reminded me that I was going to grow old and die" (11).

The only member of the family to engage Archer's sympathy is Sampson's daughter, Miranda. Largely because of her familial situation, Miranda Sampson at twenty is uncertain of herself, given to dramatic poses, impulsive actions, and psychobabble explanations of life and love. She is to Archer a young woman who has "nearly everything and could develop into nearly anything" (111). Her personality has dark edges, as she intimates in justifying her reckless driving: "I do it when I'm bored. I pretend to myself I'm going to meet something—something utterly new. Something naked and bright, a moving target in the road" (111). Miranda Sampson also possesses a freshly burgeoning sexuality to which Archer is reluctantly drawn and which Miranda herself struggles to understand. It places her at the apex of an erotic triangle that will result in the murder of her father. In her uncertain and insecure way, Miranda desires Alan Taggert, who is decidedly uninterested in her; she is decidedly uninterested in Albert Graves, of whom Archer perceives "at forty he was drunk with love" (23). Archer also perceives the relations among these three characters, when Graves "gave her a hurt look. She was looking at Taggert. Taggert was looking nowhere in particular. It was a triangle, but not an equilateral one" (23).

Both Alan Taggert and Albert Graves are carefully drawn characters. Taggert, the tall, handsome pilot, has never readjusted to a civilian life devoid of the excitement and glamour of war, and he chafes under the gruff condescension and drunken sentimentality of his employer. The inside man in the kidnapping, Taggert has the superficial charm of the man inured to death. As he prepares to kill Archer, Taggert shows him "the face of a new kind of man, calm and unfrightened, because he laid no special value on human life. Boyish and rather innocent, because he could do evil almost without knowing it. He was the kind of man who had grown up and found himself in war" (185). Albert Graves, in contrast, pulled himself out of poverty by hard work and resolute will. As Archer says, "all his life he'd been setting his mind on things—and getting them" (24). Graves also "inherited the Midwestern dream—which included the daughter of a Texas oil millionaire" (24). To reify that dream, to get Miranda Sampson, Graves kills Taggert as the pilot is about to shoot Archer—a killing Archer sees as "a justifiable homicide and something more" (241). That something more leads Graves, on the day he marries Miranda, to kill her father.

Graves is a figure of potential tragedy, a point made by the D.A. to the skeptical Archer. "A good man," Graves had "worked hard all his life, and the whole thing suddenly went sour. It lost its meaning for him. There was no more virtue or justice, in him or in the world" (244). Archer tries to insist that Graves was simply ambitious and greedy, but he finally abandons the argument, and the question remains unresolved, for the reader if not for Archer. This is the first important instance of Macdonald's refusing to tie up neatly all the loose ends of his narrative and to suggest that Archer sees what he does because of his character and his involvement with the other characters in the novel. In this case, Archer abandons the question of Graves's motivation because the subject is abstract and, like much of what he has seen from the opening pages, unreal. "I could see all the lights of the city. They didn't seem quite real. The stars and the house lights were firefly gleams, sparks of cold fire suspended in the black void. The real thing in my world was the girl beside me, warm and shuddering and lost" (245).

The final page of the novel expresses the attitude that will inform Lew Archer's actions through another eighteen novels. For all the ideas treated in the Archer novels, for all the sociological and psychological issues they raise, the primary object of Archer's concern is the individual human being. In *The Far Side of the Dollar*, written twenty years later, Archer voices the same concern: "I guess I've never been able to see much in the world besides the people in it."[16]

While superior to anything Macdonald had done before, *The Moving Target* is not without flaws. The explanation for two murders is essentially tacked onto rather than revealed by the plot. And the final assessment of Albert Graves contains notions at once extrinsic to and more interesting than the central themes of the novel. The debt to Chandler is large and obvious, in the characterization of underworld types as well as in the few instances of humor. In his next several novels, Macdonald would continue to labor under Chandler's influence, developing his craft until he was ready to express his own vision, to abandon the mean streets in which Marlowe wandered so well for the lanes of suburbia, to eschew tales of professional criminals for the stories of middle class families and the dreams and nightmares of their lives, to take the American detective story into new territory—the territory he first staked out in *The Moving Target*.

Chapter Four
Mastering the Form

From *The Drowning Pool* through *The Barbarous Coast,* Macdonald in the early and middle 1950s explored the possibilities of the genre in which he had chosen to work. The novels of this period are imbued with the ambience and some of the attitudes that Chandler had established as standard in the form, but if they derive from Chandler, they are informed by an intelligence and charged with a linguistic facility that elevate them well above most other efforts in the form. And while Macdonald labored in Chandler's extensive shadow, he also carefully probed the American detective novel, bringing to it new themes and ideas, experimenting with structure and technique, discovering by trial and error his way out from under that shadow. What he was moving toward, of course, was himself—his own fictional imperatives. Because of this experimentation, and because what he learned from Chandler sometimes failed to cohere with what he was discovering, this early work is uneven. Still, as he felt his way toward his own vision and a narrative structure to express it, Macdonald produced several novels that hold up well.

Descent into the Underworld

The Drowning Pool (1950), which Macdonald later admitted was not a major advance over *The Moving Target,*[1] is in some ways one of his more interesting early efforts. In it he introduced several of the themes that would become central to the later works, and for the first time he integrated two distinct plot lines and worked with a structure of parallel situations and characters. He also broadened the social backdrop of the action, which afforded the opportunity for a few satirical sallies that complemented his Chandlerian commentary on the ills and idiocies of his time.

The Drowning Pool begins as a poison-pen case. Archer is hired by Maude Slocum to discover the identity and to silence the author of a letter to her husband, a letter that puts him in the role of "complaisant cuckold."[2] Archer perceives that Maude is a woman deeply divided. Her blue eyes look "with a sort of double vision. They saw you clearly, took you in completely, and at the same time looked beyond you" (3). This bifurcation manifests itself in her attitude, as she guiltily evades questions about whether she is having an affair but insists that she wants to protect her marriage and family. Yet Archer's initial reservations about her are transformed into sympathy when he comes to understand the affectional and psychosexual chaos of her situation.

The Slocums—Maude; her husband, James; and their sixteen-year-old daughter, Cathy—live in Nopal Valley with his wealthy mother, who keeps the family on an allowance. James Slocum is an effete, affected, and sexually ambivalent aesthete. Cathy is an intelligent girl disturbed by the tangle of sexual relations that she senses in and around her family, and by her own sexual impulses. Olivia Slocum, James's mother, holds her son's family in economic bondage, while she herself is bound by twin obsessions. As Archer observes, "she was fixed on her own lost beauty, and couldn't grow old or let her son grow up" (42); at the same time Archer finds "a little frightening" (44) the intensity of her feeling for her ranch, which she romanticizes as an island of pristine beauty in an area experiencing a rapid and ugly alteration brought about by the oil industry, and on which she refuses to allow oil exploration. Thus the world Archer finds himself in pulsates with the energies of "sex and money: the forked root of evil" (11).

The first third of the novel concentrates on the Slocums, their fiercely confused feelings for one another and their relations with others—Maude's tense yet ambiguous relationship with Sheriff Ralph Knudson, her husband's friendship with the effeminate British poet and playwright Francis Marvell, and her daughter's involvement with chauffeur Pat Reavis. Cathy Slocum also has intense and apparently incestuous feelings for her father, at the same time that her mother appears to be encouraging her toward intimacy with Knudson. This snakes' nest of emotions Macdonald places within a posturing group of small-town aesthetes, set against a background of raw oil-town greed that despoils the land as it corrupts its inhabitants.

In depicting the social and economic background of the action, Macdonald follows Chandler's lead, offering both cynical summations—"There was nothing wrong with Southern California that a rise in the ocean level wouldn't cure" (26)—as well as descriptions that combine savage lyricism with acerbic social criticism, as in Archer's first view of Nopal Valley, "oil-pumps nodding and clanking where cattle had grazed," a town that had "grown enormously, like a tumor" and "thrust out shoots in all directions." The town Archer sees is all "raw new housing developments and the real estate shacks to go with them, a half-mile gauntlet of one-story buildings along the highway," and a "bowling alley wide enough to house a B-36. . . . A quiet town in a sunny valley had hit the jackpot hard, and didn't know what to do with itself at all" (26–27).

Narrowing his focus, Macdonald also satirically skewers the pretensions of the provincial artsy set, first when Archer watches a rehearsal of Marvell's play—"the kind of stuff that parodied itself. Phony sophistication with a high gloss, and no insides at all" (19)—and later at a cocktail party, where the conversation ranges from André Gide to Albert Schweitzer but the dominant subject is sex: "Sex solo, in duet, trio, quartet; for all-male chorus; for choir and symphony; and played on the harpsichord in three-fourths time" (50).

Near the end of this party, however, Archer observes the ominous gathering of Ralph Knudson, Maude Slocum, and her husband: "Short of homicidal violence, the atmosphere around the piano was as ugly as I had ever seen" (52). Soon the atmosphere is in fact homicidal, as Olivia Slocum's body is pulled from the swimming pool.

Here the narrative shifts both direction and focus. In pursuit of Pat Reavis, the obvious suspect in Olivia Slocum's murder, Archer descends into the tawdry and violent underside of Nopal Valley and Los Angeles, finally finding himself in a confrontation with Walter Kilbourne, a former thug and now the owner of an oil company. With help from Kilbourne's wife, Mavis, Archer begins to make connections. Violence increases, as Reavis is murdered and Maude Slocum kills herself; a series of reversals sends Archer careening between the Valley and Los Angeles, subjected to threats, assaults, bribes, and attempted drowning in a hydrotherapy chamber, which results instead in Mavis Kilbourne shooting her husband. Most of the violence is the product of Kilbourne's attempt to gain access to the Slocum land for oil drilling, but the narrative comes full circle with the revelations that Knudson is Cathy's natural father and that the girl killed her grandmother. Knowledge of this killing led Maude Slocum to suicide. The novel ends as Archer agrees to remain silent and let Knudson take his daughter away.

All of this is well handled, especially the mirroring of the marital situations of Maude Slocum and Mavis Kilbourne and drawing clear thematic implications in the different attitudes of the two women. There is a problem, however. Archer's adventures in the underworld are but superficially connected to the drama within the Slocum family. Because Archer's—and Macdonald's—real interest is the Slocums, the last two-thirds of the novel, for all the action it contains, seems static, less energized and intense than the first section. This split also affects the development of the central theme. The novel's titular image appears as Archer kisses Mavis Kilbourne: "I drew back from the whirling vortex that had opened, the drowning pool" (119). In this novel most of the characters are caught up in a sexual maelstrom, the pull of which Archer himself must resist. But the emotional and moral center of the novel is Maude Slocum and her conflicting passions, her struggle with love and duty, desire and obligation. After placing Maude and her predicament in the forefront of our concern, however, Macdonald largely abandons her for excursions into the criminal milieu. Thus *The Drowning Pool* has a fractured feel to it, as if Macdonald began by writing from his own imagination only to retreat to the safety of the generically conventional.

This retreat from himself and his subject took Macdonald through his next two novels. Interestingly enough, however, although—or perhaps because—they contain little of himself but instead delve deeply into the standard material of the genre, they are two of his stronger books. Certainly in *The Way Some People Die* and *The Ivory Grin* Macdonald does more with this material, and does it better, than anyone except Chandler ever managed.

The Way Some People Die (1951) is structured to produce unusual effects. It begins as a missing person case, but the young woman Archer is hired to find, Galatea (Galley) Lawrence, appears a quarter of the way through the book; at that point, the mystery becomes not her whereabouts but her essence. It is a mystery that Archer never solves. Before they meet, he has collected varying reports on the character of the woman in whose photograph he has seen a beauty both "passionate and bold."[3] As the action proceeds and he tries to fit what he has been told with the young woman he observes, Archer finds himself both attracted to and in sympathy with Galley, despite his growing suspicion of her guilt. At the end of the novel, after he has threatened, cajoled, and tricked her into the admission that she murdered three men, he is still unable to explain her actions. In a long confrontation scene, Archer reconstructs the murders and tentatively assigns as motive everything from love to greed to sociopathology, but finally nothing accounts for her actions or overcomes his feeling for her. In the final pages, he finds himself compromised and compromising, leaving with Galley's mother a stolen thirty thousand dollars—evidence against Galley that her mother ironically plans to use to defend her—at the same time that he acknowledges, "I knew that Galley Lawrence was guilty as hell" (245).

If Archer's investigation of the evil infecting Galley Lawrence leads him to the impasse of the inexplicable, the rest of the novel lays out in precise detail the world into which she descended. As Archer searches first for Galley, and then for the human meaning of her actions, he wends his way through the seamy side of Southern California, from the estate fortress of the mob boss to the motel of the junkie and the hooker, over a landscape of plastic and grime peopled with predators and their prey, through the world of wrestling and pinball rackets, dope and prostitution. With deft strokes Macdonald cuts through the bluff and bluster of the denizens of this nightmare world to reveal their true and truly human natures. There is mob kingpin Danny Dowser, who "had a quality of unacted violence that held the attention" (38), but, as Archer later understands, "Dowser was afraid to die, and I realized why he couldn't bear to be left alone" (97). Or the heroin pusher Mosquito, of whom Archer says, "The red corridor light shone down on him like a dirty little sun scaled to the world in his head" (181). Mostly, however, what Archer meets in this world are its victims—the poor and the young, the fearful and the hopeless, the foolish and the unfortunate. In such a world, Galley Lawrence, evil though she may be, stands out "like a chicken hawk in a flock of pullets" (10).

"It's sort of sad" about Galley, Archer says. "All that energy and ingenuity wasted" (238). And the overriding effect of the novel is a similar sadness at the waste of human energies and aspirations. As Archer cannot satisfactorily explain why Galley Lawrence acts as she does, neither can he neatly classify the other characters as good or evil, for in this world both good and evil arise from the same sources: fear, loneliness, the longing for love, the easy errors of human weakness.

Love in the Gutter

The best of the early Archer novels, *The Ivory Grin* (1952) is also set in the criminal world. This time, however, Macdonald's subject is not the professional but the intimate activities of the lawless. Fusing some of his own interests with those dominant in the genre, Macdonald probes the dank recesses of the criminal psyche. The plotting is ingenious, as one case turns into another, seemingly minor characters become central, suspicion shifts as suspense mounts, and the action swirls around a character who never appears. During the course of this action, Archer's own sense of culpability steadily deepens the foreboding that hovers over his pursuit of the truth, a pursuit that leads from revelation to reversal to a tragic conclusion. As he would do in the later novels, in *The Ivory Grin* Archer follows a helical path, circling through postwar Southern California, from the ghettos of sun-baked valley towns to the hilltop domains of long-established wealth to a rented mansion that "was Spanish Renaissance with a strong Inquisitional hangover,"[4] while at the same time he descends into the past to uncover the links of love that give meaning to the violence and suffering in the present.

Two-thirds of the way through the novel, as Archer argues with a Bella City policeman about the guilt of a murder suspect, he makes a decision: "I had been trying to decide all morning whether to give Brake everything I knew. I decided not to. The frayed ends of several lives . . . were braided into the case. The pattern I was picking out strand by strand was too complicated to be explained in the language of physical evidence" (148). So complex is this pattern that even at this point Archer cannot perceive its organizing principle. But it has been that way from the beginning.

Against his better judgment, Archer has accepted an assignment to locate in Bella City a young black nurse named Lucy Champion and to report on her movements. His reservations are prompted not by the job but by his employer, a fiftyish, beringed, but vaguely androgynous woman calling herself Una Larkin, whose obvious prevarications seem to stem from her character: "It was like talking to several persons at once, none of them quite complete" (4). Yet these several personalities combine in an indomitable will: "Her walk was the shortest distance between things she wanted" (10).

In Bella City, a "sprawling dusty town" in which "the highway was a rough social equator bisecting the community into lighter and darker hemispheres" (11), Archer quickly locates Lucy Champion, whom he follows first to the ghetto home of Mrs. Ann Norris and her son Alex, where Lucy has rented a room, and then to a motel from which Archer calls his employer. Una comes to the motel, has a conversation with Lucy, which Archer overhears but does not completely understand, and leaves. Continuing his surveillance, Archer tracks Lucy to the office of Dr. Samuel Benning, where he speaks with nurse's aid Florida Gutierrez, and with Mrs. Benning, a "tall black-haired woman" whose "beauty canceled the room" (31). Lucy then leads Archer to the railroad station, where he encounters Max Heiss, an alcoholic private detective who "had taken a running jump at manhood and still, at forty or forty-five, had never quite got his hands on it" (32). Heiss, who is also following Lucy, knows that Archer has been hired by Una; telling Archer "I bet you don't even know what case you're on" (34), Heiss offers to share the case and the "great deal of money in it" (35). As Archer rejects the offer, Lucy suddenly escapes from both detectives. Archer returns to the motel, where he finds Lucy with her throat cut. In her purse is a newspaper clipping about the disappearance of Charles Singleton, Jr., scion of a wealthy family in nearby Arroyo Beach.

In fewer than forty pages, Macdonald presents the characters and issues that he will examine in more depth over the rest of the novel and places them in a vividly rendered environment. But as Archer's investigation concentrates not on "physical evidence" but on the murk of human motive, so Macdonald creates a world of impressionistic detail. On East Hidalgo Street "housewives black, brown, and sallow were hugging parcels and pushing shopping carts on the sidewalk. Above them a ramshackle house, with paired front windows like eyes demented by earthquake memories, advertised Rooms for Transients on one side, Palm Reading on the other. A couple of Mexican children, boy and girl, strolled by hand in hand in a timeless noon on their way to an early marriage" (12). In the neighborhood of Ann Norris and her son Alex, "in the photographic light the wretchedness of the houses had a stern kind of clarity or beauty, like old men's faces in the sun" (14). The motel in which Lucy is killed "stood in the social badlands between the highway and the railroad tracks" (22). In the house where Dr. Benning has both his office and his home, Archer finds himself in what had been "the front parlor of the house. Its present quality was a struggling lack of respectability . . . it was a room in which the crime of poverty had left clues" (30). This postwar Southern California is like Archer's motel room, where people "had lain alone or in pairs on the iron bed and looked at the yellow ceiling. Traces of their dirt remained in the corners, their odors clung to the walls. They had come from all over the country to look at the yellow ceiling, stir in the iron bed, finger the walls and leave their indelible marks" (25). It is these "indelible marks" that lead Archer to the ultimate meaning of the story

Archer quickly finds more of these marks. Alex Norris is blamed for Lucy Champion's death, but Archer, urged on by both his conviction that Alex is innocent and his awareness that in allowing Lucy to escape he himself is not without guilt, sets out after the truth. He confronts Una, who "in red Japanese pajamas . . . looked less like a woman than a scxlcss imp who had grown old in hell" (57), but he learns little; he listens as Max Heiss tries to pump information from Florrie Gutierrez, until she is taken away by Mrs. Benning; and he breaks into Dr. Benning's office, where he discovers a wired and tagged anatomical skeleton grinning "the ivory grin of death" (74) and is himself discovered by Mrs. Benning, who "can talk different ways, depending on who I'm talking to" (76). Then, following a road that "ascended hills terraced like the steps of an easy manmade purgatory" (80), he drives to the Singleton estate, in a neighborhood that was an "earthly paradise where money begot plants upon property. People were irrelevant, unless they happened to have money or property" (81). Talking with Mrs. Singleton about the disappearance of her son, Charles, Archer concludes that "the situation was too complicated for me to understand or try to deal with." (87). Before he leaves, however, he is hired by Sylvia Treen, Mrs. Singleton's young paid companion, to pursue the case, and he learns that both Max Heiss and Lucy Champion had been to the Singleton house and that Charles Singleton had left with "a tall woman with yellow hair, and very beautiful" (92).

Tracing the curious connections among the dead Lucy Champion, the missing Charles Singleton, Jr., and the mysterious blond woman, Archer discovers that all three are linked with Una, whose last name is really Durano.

Soon he finds himself at another huge old house, where he sees at a barred window a man "trying to wrench the bars out of their concrete sockets. Each time he tried and failed, he said one word in a low growling guttural. "'Hell,' he said. 'Hell. Hell'" (111). Then Archer witnesses a bizarre scene in which the same man, Una's brother Leo, first spews forth a stream of obscene and insane mutterings and then shoots both Una and an orderly with a cap pistol. Wearily, Archer decides "to call it a day" (117).

As the plot pulls Archer through a succession of encounters with the other characters, structural parallels expose deeper aspects of theme. The two big houses are linked by death: the one rented by the Duranos abuts on a cemetery, where "stone angels pointed at the sky; saints spread their arms in iron benediction" (110), and Archer's description of it is studded with infernal images. Similar images occur in his description of the neighborhood of the Singleton home, and the drive leading to the house is lined by "yews like honorary pallbearers" (81). Both poor, black Mrs. Ann Norris and wealthy, white Mrs. Singleton are widows whose nearly obsessive concern is the fate of their only sons—fates for which the two mothers are partially responsible. The two nurses, Lucy Champion and Florida Gutierrez, are antithetical figures—the dead nurse having been strong and honest, the living one weak of spirit and conscience. The missing Charles Singleton, Jr. is loved by both Sylvia Treen and the unidentified blonde woman. Even Archer has his counterpart in the disreputable and scheming Max Heiss. As his private detective and narrator assess these characters, Macdonald carefully juxtaposes scenes to broaden the thematic relevance of specific situations and to connect the different social levels with the strands of human fallibility and love that Archer unravels.

Little in *The Ivory Grin,* then, is as it first appears. This is especially true of the characters. Mrs. Norris, for example, seems upon first meeting the stereotypical "churchy" (19) black woman bound up in a rigid religiosity that manifests itself primarily in an angry scrutiny of anything smacking of sexual impropriety. When she meets Archer later, however, her rectitude is revealed to be a complex construct of guilt and compassion, fear and love. Of her treatment of Lucy, she confesses, "I made a mistake. I rose up in anger against her. She had no safe place to go. If I'd known what was going to come to her, she could have stayed on with us" (134). Her concern, she explains, was "keeping my name respectable," but almost immediately she corrects herself: "I misstated myself. . . . It is not my name I care for. It's my son" (135). In the same way, her religious attitudes constitute not a sanctimonious sense of moral superiority but the source of a constant moral struggle. Responding to Archer's inquiries about Dr. Benning and his wife, she tells him, "She was a

Jezebel to him, a blonde Jezebel mistreating him without shame. It ended as I expected with her running off and divorcing him," but she again immediately stops herself: "I ought to wash out my mouth, repeating gossip and scandal on the Lord's Day" (136). Finally Archer comes to see her as "a black Rachel lamenting the wrecked hopes of all mothers for their sons, black and white and tan" (141).

As Archer's inquiry slowly uncovers the humanity of Mrs. Norris, his successive encounters with Dr.Benning lead to a quite different discovery. When Archer first sees Benning in his Hildago Street office, he notes the doctor's "pale worried eyes. Deep lines of sorrow dragged down from the wings of his vulnerable nose" (32). At their next meeting, Benning greets Archer with "the air of a beaten old man" (126), but he explains Lucy Champion's "psychosomatic" ills with sympathy and compassion, and at City Hall he attempts to console Mrs. Norris. Later, however, finding Archer with his wife Benning responds with hysterical bible-thumping—"You had your hands on her. Carnal knowledge" (174)—and Archer perceives that "he was the suicidal man who never quite nerved himself to suicide" (174). Slowly Archer uncovers the real Dr. Benning, a man who reacts to the disdain of his wife by "slipping rung by rung into a hell of self-abasement" (175). Not until their final meeting does Archer see the ultimate ground of that abasement, or understand its cause; when Benning cries, "Why do you hate me?" Archer observes, "He wasn't asking me alone. He was asking all the people who had known him and not loved him in his life" (238).

If Archer's exposure of Dr. Benning is a gradual unwinding of a sheet of pathetic respectability wrapped around the doctor's mummified heart, his discovery of Mrs. Benning's tortured humanity is sudden and dramatic, turning the entire case, and the meaning of the action, upside down. As the strands of the case unravel and its pattern becomes discernible, Archer can tell the policeman Brake, "Mrs. Benning is the central figure in the picture" (192). She is also, under her dyed hair, the "beautiful blonde" Bess Wionowski, the apparent source of the evil that has resulted in the deaths of Charles Singleton, Max Heiss, and Lucy Champion, as well as in the misery in which most of the other characters have been immersed.

Through most of the novel, Elizabeth Benning seems just another version of the stereotyped femme fatale of the American detective novel, the beautiful, amoral, coldly sensuous woman who preys on the sexual and sympathetic impulses of men to get what she wants—Velma Valento/Mrs. Grayle in Chandler's *Farewell, My Lovely* is an obvious model. While Archer's dealings with the other characters steadily uncover a human reality masked by layers of pretense, his meetings with Elizabeth Benning serve only to confirm his initial evaluation. He quickly detects, through her speech and attitudes, the influence of the "hard school" from which she admits with "queer pride" that she "graduated with honors" (169). She attempts to thwart Archer's inquiries with sex—"I turned, softly ambushed by her hips" (171)—and a highly edited story of her life, both of which work to reinforce his original assessment. For the other characters too she is an obvious type, which they indicate by their derogatory epithets—"Jezebel," "beast," "pipperino." Even as the spiral of circumstances narrows and Archer comes to see more clearly her centrality in the case, his view of her remains unchanged.

In the novel's penultimate and climactic chapter, however, when Archer captures Mrs. Benning in his office, he finds a much different woman: "Her past was coming out on her face like latent handwriting. . . . Dissolution was working in her rapidly like a fatal disease she had caught from her husband that day" (223–24). Yet Archer's rather simpleminded moralism does not account for the woman. As Elizabeth Benning answers his questions, she slowly becomes Bess Wionowski, and Archer is forced to revise his judgment. The story that emerges is harrowingly human and touched with tragedy. It is a story of love and betrayal, violence and despair, its theme a problem that plagues the human heart and that afflicts most of the other characters in the novel: "The people you love are never the ones that love you" (230).

The only character about whom Archer's view does not change is Una Durano. In fact, Archer can never quite get at her essence. As he could not explain Galley Lawrence's evil, neither can he understand Una's. The obvious explanations—greed, the drive for power—do not account for her thoroughgoing malevolence. Archer ventures metaphoric assessments, most of which are sexually and eschatologically oriented—"she looked fifty, in spite of the girlishness and the boyishness. Americans never grew old: they died; and her eyes had guilty knowledge of it" (4). At the end, however, he can ascribe the source of evil only to an insanity she shares with her brother: "Her eyes were blind with the same darkness I had seen on her brother's face. The gun in her hand was real" (232). Archer cannot fire his own gun in time to save Bess, but when he does, he shoots "to kill" (232).

Moral monster that she is, however, Una has not killed Charles Singleton, Lucy Champion, or Max Heiss. The murderer is Dr. Samuel Benning. Archer is quick to link the doctor's actions with the evil that poisoned the air around Una Durano: "It's the human idea you've been butchering and boiling down and trying to burn away. You can't stand the human idea. You and Una Durano don't stack up against it, and you know it" (239). But again Archer's moralistic judgment does not hold; there is a quick reversal, as Macdonald gives Dr. Benning the final lines of dialogue: "I do feel grief for her. I loved her. There was nothing I wouldn't do" (240). Archer has solved the case. He has identified the murderer of Lucy Champion and Max Heiss, and he has found Charles Singleton, Jr. (He had found him long before the end of the novel, of course—or what was left of him: the skeleton in Benning's closet grinning the "ivory grin of death.") He has watched Bess die, and he has killed Una. All the strands of the case have unraveled, the tangle of love and betrayal and guilt and greed have smoothed into discernible motive. But motive is not explanation. What prompts these emotions, heats and twists and tempers them into implements of death? Why do people love as they do? Archer doesn't know. The mystery remains.

Paperbacks and Problems

Macdonald rightly believed that *The Ivory Grin* was his best book to date.[5] He did not follow it with another Archer novel, however; *Meet Me at the Morgue* (1953) is instead narrated by probation officer Howard Cross, who is also the central character. This is what created the difficulties that wreaked havoc on the pre-Archer novels. By this time Macdonald had developed the narrative skill to deal more effectively with this situation, and his characterization of Cross is considerably less heroic than that of the pre-Archer narrators; Cross in fact resembles Archer in attitude and investigative method. Like Archer, Cross attends more to the other characters than to himself, so that the mystery in which they are involved is unobscured by his own inner life. Unfortunately for the novel as a whole, Macdonald combines a complex detective plot with Cross's romance with the mother of a young kidnapping victim; because the narrative focuses on the intricacies of the detective story, the love story seems superficial and gratuitous.

Meet Me at the Morgue represents a step backward in Macdonald's development, but much in the novel is well done—the prose is vivid, the action is charged with suspense, the characters are whole and human. One of these, a seedy but honest private investigator named Bourke, is of special interest. Macdonald told Hugh Kenner he used Cross as the narrator so that he could present an objective view of Bourke, who is "Archer, seen from the outside."[6] It is a view that critics given to saintly adjectives when discussing Archer might attend to.

Like Archer, Bourke gets most of his income from divorce cases, the attendant temptations of which have resulted in his being left by his wife. "With quick suspicious Hollywood eyes set on ball bearings in an anxious face" (88), Bourke strikes Howard Cross as a "hungry barracuda wearing a bow tie" (89). (Archer's evaluations of his own reflection throughout the early novels are strikingly similar.) And while Cross can tell an FBI man that Bourke "seems legitimate," he accepts the agent's assertion that "you never can tell about these private operators. The dirt they work in is always rubbing off on them" (94)—Archer says much the same thing in Macdonald's next novel, in fact. For all his oft-remarked compassion, Lew Archer remains a man whose moral assessments must be understood in the context of his environment and his own sometimes questionable actions.

Macdonald's tenth novel is less significant for its art than for the reception the book received from his publisher. Before accepting the manuscript, Knopf sent it to Pocket Books, the paperback house; their complaints that it lacked action and a sharp Chandlerian distinction between good and evil, and their impertinent suggestion that Knopf's editorial staff might rewrite some of the book, both angered and depressed Macdonald, and spurred him to a spirited, perhaps even savage defense.

In a letter to Knopf,[7] Macdonald combined criticism of Chandler and Mickey Spillane with a forceful statement of his own attitudes and aspirations. Acknowledging Chandler's "power" and influence—"Hell, he's one of my masters"—Macdonald rejected his "vision of good and evil. It seems to me that it is conventional to the point of old-maidishness, that it is antihuman to the point of sadism (Chandler hates all women, and really likes only old men, boys, and his Marlowe *persona*)." His own subject, he said, was "human error," his interest "the exploration of lives," his theme "exploitation": "But even the murderers in the last five books have seemed more human than 'bad' to me. I would rather understand them than condemn them. I would rather display them in characteristic poses and sum up their lives and the reasons for their lives than cause a self-righteous hero to denounce them or push them around for the sake of action."

Of Spillane and paperback publishers he was disdainful, insisting that "the Spillane phenomenon, which hasn't much to do with the mystery as such but which probably has a lot to do with paperback publishers' notions of what a good mystery should be," was an aberration. "The old-line hardboiled mystery, with many guns and fists and fornications, has been ruined by its own practitioners, including Chandler. Spillane pulled the plug. I refuse to follow it down the drain." In his own work, his "hope has been to write 'popular' novels which would not be inferior to 'serious' novels," "to improve the form, and to write real novels in it," and "to make [it] literate, humane, and let us face it, adult."

The letter to Knopf, with all its obvious frustration and barely restrained rage, and especially its attack on Chandler—we do not need to invoke

Harold Bloom to explain Macdonald's "misreading" of one of his "masters"—was in fact Macdonald's literary manifesto. What it manifested were his ideas about the direction the American detective novel should take and who was best qualified to lead it in that direction. It is an expression not only of anger but also of ambition. As Chandler had single-handedly rescued the hardboiled detective novel from breast-and-bullet hacks of the 1930s and 1940s, so Macdonald would save it from Chandler's inept imitators and Spillane's pathological machismo. Rather than a repository for the sex and violence of juvenile male fantasy, the form to Macdonald was "a convention or structure with which almost anything could be done, a technique both difficult and free." And he would effect this second rescue of the American detective novel by "developing my own point of view and craft and technique to the limit." What is remarkable about this manifesto is its prescience, for Macdonald was to accomplish precisely the task he set for himself.

But not immediately. Although he returned to Archer in the next novel, *Find a Victim* (1954), he again had problems with Knopf and was forced to revise the manuscript. Macdonald's friend Anthony Boucher in the *New York Times Book Review* described the novel as "a strange and haunting blend of professional crime and private complexities . . . that seems to me to belong to an entirely different genre of its own."[8] Strange and haunting it is. But rather than belonging to a different genre, the novel is an example of what happens when "private complexities" are of such imaginative strength as to overwhelm the "professional" behavior of both detective and author.

The characters and issues at the center of *Find a Victim* are the most deeply felt and powerfully realized of all those in Macdonald's early fiction. But he has a long hard time getting to this center. The early chapters seem almost a parody of the Spillane–Pocket Book formula, as Archer finds a dying young man along a highway, muscles his way into the case under the dual impetus of an obscurely private morality and a sentimental romantic attachment, rejects the sexual overtures of hookers and housewives, and pugnaciously confronts local law enforcement officers. His primary investigative method is eavesdropping, as he skulks around doors and windows to overhear conversations that he takes to be of great import but that logically can have no meaning to him at the moment. For a writer with ten novels under his belt, it is a curiously amateurish performance.

Macdonald recognized the novel's deficiencies, years later noting that *Find a Victim* is "too action-fraught . . . but I think the last couple of chapters rise to the wholly human."[9] In these final chapters, after dispensing with the hoods in a shoot-out-at-the-OK-garage, Macdonald finally gets to his true subject, the tortured relations within a tragically twisted family. As

Archer sorts through the acts and emotions of the Meyer family—the widowed father, the two daughters, and the elder daughter's husband—he discovers human horrors beside which the criminality in the preceding chapters pales into relative insignificance. Incest and murder, love and guilt and madness bind the Meyer family together as they tear its members apart. Exploring the evil that issues from these tormented psyches, however, Archer discovers no evildoers. He finds only victims.

As Jerry Speir has observed,[10] most of these victims are women—the Meyer sisters, to be sure, but also most of the other female characters. The world of *Find a Victim* pulses with sexual predation; it is a world in which women can survive only by themselves becoming predators, victimizers, and murderers. Macdonald makes this clear in a number of ways. Archer, for example, explains that "this state is crawling with easy-money boys. . . . They prey on women. As long as women own three fourths of the property in this country, there will be men trying to take it away from them, and succeeding."[11] The notion is echoed by Hilda Church: "Most of the men in this city are barbarians where women are concerned" (48). Macdonald reinforces this view by placing on either side of the Meyer family the Kerrigans and the MacGowans. Kate Kerrigan has an "oblique blond beauty" (21) and a philandering husband. After seven years of suffering in a bad marriage, Kate is caught in a sexual trap, able neither to love her husband nor to let him go. Kerrigan is, according to Archer, one of those men with "nothing in them but hunger, a hungry hole you can't fill" (162). One of the women he turns to is Jo MacGowan Summer, "as full of sex as a grape is full of juice, and so young it hadn't begun to sour" (24). Growing up on the streets, Jo learned to use sex for both pleasure and advancement of a singing career, only to discover that the men she was involved with, like the three hoods who rape her, "never showed proper respect for *my* human life" (182).

Between these poles of sexual suffering reside the Meyer family. The father, "a big old wreck of a man" (37), lives in "the kind of room you find in back-country ranch-houses where old men hold the last frontier against women and civilization and hygiene" (39). He is a man who can get angry with his dying wife because the child she has just given birth to is not a son, and fifteen years later sexually assault that child because "I couldn't stop myself. You don't know how it was, being without a woman all those years" (142). The girl, Anne, grows up like Jo MacGowan Summer, wild and independent, taking her sexual pleasures where she chooses. When she makes the mistake of taking her brother-in-law as a lover, it gets her killed. But when Archer discovers Anne's killer, and the killer of two men, he finds not a villain but another victim, Anne's sister Hilda Meyer Church.

In Hilda the sexual dreams entertained by the other characters are transformed into perpetual nightmare. Growing up with a bestial father, desperate to protect and to believe in the sexual innocence of her sister, Hilda was emotionally disturbed long before her marriage. An early and unwanted pregnancy led to a suicide attempt, but after losing the child Hilda improved and settled into her marriage to Brandon Church and the safety it provided from her psyche-ravaging fears. It did not, however, free her to love, so that she condemned her husband to an empty life. After nine years in which he "kept her living along like a fairly normal person," Brandon Church finally "failed her" (211) and turned to her sister. Hilda also turned to her sister, with a gun.

Sexual themes inform *Find a Victim,* shaping its characters and driving its action. Even Archer rides a crest of sexual desire, for his continued activity in the case is largely the result of his growing attraction to Kate Kerrigan. The crucial relationship in the novel, however, is not sexual but fraternal. As the story unfolds, the character with whom Archer is most intensely engaged is Sheriff Brandon Church. Archer's confrontations with Church grow steadily more violent, as the detective discovers the depth of the sheriff's complicity in hijacking and murder. In several powerful scenes the two exchange threats, accusations, and finally blows, until Archer discovers the truth: "My judgment of Church had been turned upside down in the last few minutes. He had broken some of the rules. His life had been disordered and passionate. But he was an honest man, according to his lights. 'I'd have done the same,' I said" (209).

As Peter Wolfe has astutely observed, Church and Archer stand in dialectical tension with one another, functioning as different sides of the same character.[12] Archer's initial suspicion of and antagonism toward the sheriff develop into a moral and professional anger that drives the detective to a single-minded, nearly obsessive stripping away of Church's evasions, subterfuges, and lies to expose the true nature of his character and guilt. Stunningly, ironically, what Archer finds is himself.

For all its dramatic power and movingly portrayed characters, *Find a Victim* remains one of Macdonald's less artistically successful novels. If it recovers from the ineptitude of its opening chapters, it can neither escape the conventionalities of its hijacking plot nor relate that plot other than superficially to the primary sexual theme. But it at least resolves the hijacking plot. Archer's relationship with Kate Kerrigan, which develops over the first half of the novel, is in the second simply abandoned as the action tracks away from Archer's personal sexual dream to the nightmares of the Meyer family. The result is a novel of gripping pieces.

On the Edge

Of his next novel, *The Barbarous Coast* (1956), Macdonald said, "I was getting myself and my form under more personal control. It was my largest book so far, in both social range and moral complexity. In it I was learning to get rid of the protective wall between my mind and the perilous stuff of my own life" (*SP*, 37). All these claims the novel itself verifies. At the same time, it makes clear that he had taken as far as he could the American detective novel as he had learned it from Chandler.

Certainly of a broader "social range and moral complexity" than anything he had done, *The Barbarous Coast* nevertheless demonstrates the limits of the American detective novel after Chandler. The division of society into haves and have-nots, and of morality into good guys and bad guys, allowed Chandler to make powerful distinctions. But as there is no middle ground in his morality, so there is no middle class in his society. Chandler's art is one of absolutes and extremes, as is that of those who strove to imitate his considerable success. Macdonald's main interests, however, lay in the burgeoning middle class, that vast group of Americans largely ignored by hardboiled detective writers. This middle class in the 1950s enjoyed postwar affluence if not wealth, established suburbia if not community, and espoused moralism to replace a system of values lost in war, social mobility, and the pursuit of the consumer version of the American dream. Addressing this subject required a form quite different from the one Chandler had devised. Macdonald was soon to create it, but not until he had exhausted the one he had inherited.

The Barbarous Coast is Macdonald's Hollywood novel. He had skirted the subject in several of the earlier novels, occasionally dealing with characters attached to the film industry, and regularly allowing Archer to couch his observations in terms of the dream and the dreaming of Hollywood. Now he takes it up directly, placing at the center of a complex action the artificial views of reality that the film industry both purveys and feeds upon. His treatment of the subject is not radically new, but it does illustrate the extent to which Hollywood's flickering images permeate the consciousness of American society, and it nicely links the film world to its logical if extreme and corrupt projection in the Las Vegas of the mid 1950s.

It takes Macdonald a while to get to this subject, however. For the first six chapters Archer remains in and around the Channel Club, a private retreat of the affluent that lies "on a shelf of rock overlooking the sea, toward the southern end of the beach called Malibu."[13] He has been called to the club by its manager, Clarence Bassett, a prim, sixtyish man who wants protection from the young Toronto sportswriter George Wall. Wall's wife, Hester, a former employee of the club, has disappeared, for which Wall holds Bassett responsible. Archer finally agrees to search for her.

Although he does not realize it, Archer has already seen how his search will end. As Archer examines the photographs in Bassett's office, he is "stopped by one of three divers, a man and two girls, taking off in unison from the high tower. Their bodies hung clear of the tower against a light summer sky, arched in identical swan dives, caught at the height of their parabolas before gravity took hold and snatched them back to earth" (17). Archer has cause to recall the picture throughout the book, for it prefigures the fate of the three young people around whom the action of the novel revolves: Hester Campbell Wall, Gabrielle Torres, and Manuel Torres. Gabrielle has already been murdered, and both Hester and Manuel—now the aspiring actor Lance Leonard—are involved in an extortion plot that leads to their murders. All three of the former divers are driven to their death by the force of their dreams of Hollywood stardom. As Macdonald makes clear, however, this is not a simple case of the destruction of innocence by the forces of corruption and greed. Each of the three shares moral responsibility for the events that turn murderous; each has been corrupted by the dream before being destroyed by it. As Macdonald takes pains to demonstrate, this is as it must be, for the dream itself has been corrupted. "The other part" of the beach called Malibu is "practically a slum" (31). The version of *Salammbo* that Hollywood would offer would have a happy ending. Hollywood fronts for a Las Vegas skimming operation.

The plot carefully charts the depth of the influence of this dream and the source of its perversion. As in previous novels, Archer again swings between the rich—the members of the Channel Club, especially Simon Graff, head of Helio-Graff studios, and his disturbed wife, Isobel—and the underworld, here composed of studio thugs and the muscle boys of mobster Carl Stern. Establishing the connections between these societal (if not moral) poles, Archer also establishes the extent to which belief in the dream creates victims for the criminal world. No one in the novel is exempt from the suffering caused by this collusion between fantasy and avarice. Dreams of love and wealth produce only death and suffering.

The Barbarous Coast contains an observation by Lew Archer that is adduced in every extended discussion of Macdonald's fiction: "The problem was to love people, try to serve them, without wanting anything from them. I was a long way from solving that one" (119). Most critics rightly perceive this to reveal Archer's primary motivation as a man and a private investigator. It is not quite so Christ-like a musing as these critics would have it, however. It comes after Archer flees a woman to whom he is so sexually attracted that "I caught myself doubting my premises, doubting that she could be any kind of hustler. Besides, there was just enough truth in her accusation, enough cruelty in my will to justice, enough desire in my pity, to make the room uncomfortable for me" (119). Hardly altruistic, Archer's remarks rather express his inability to separate his personal and professional lives. He would love, but finally his will to love is not as strong as the "cruelty in my will to justice." Thus the absence of a real personal life. Thus the emotional intensity of his professional life.

The remark also suggests why *The Barbarous Coast* was the last novel in which Macdonald concentrated on professional criminals. Many of the characters whom Archer dealt with in these early novels are difficult to care about. While Macdonald labored to humanize them, he was sometimes unable to overcome their innate limitations as characters. Only with characters he could place in situations like those that continued to haunt him could he do what he wanted to do with the American detective novel.

With the first five Archer novels, Macdonald established himself as the most competent practitioner, besides Chandler, of the American detective novel. *The Ivory Grin* is an especially good piece of work, and *The Way Some People Die* is nearly as effective. In these and the other novels of this period, Macdonald developed his craft, bringing to largely conventional material many of the structural techniques of "serious" novels. Few of his more personal concerns appear directly in this fiction, but as he served his apprenticeship, Macdonald gave indications that he was preparing to adapt the form to the service of his own goals. He soon would, developing a fiction whose intricate combination of subject, structure, and style has come to be recognized as "quintessentially Macdonald."

Chapter Five
The Doomsters

Writing to his editor, Macdonald described his seventh Archer novel as a "culminating book" in which he "intended to close off an era . . . in the 'hardboiled' field."[1] That novel, *The Doomsters* (1958), does indeed mark the end of an era in the American detective novel, standing as the last superior effort in the Chandlerian tradition. (Chandler himself, of course, had moved beyond that tradition in 1953, with *The Long Goodbye*.) It is also the best novel Macdonald had yet written and arguably the finest novel in the strictly hardboiled manner.

A Significantly Moving Action

The Doomsters meets all the expectations we might legitimately bring to a detective novel. It poses an originally simple question that develops into a complex and multilayered mystery, the gradual illumination of which sheds light into darker recesses of character and subtle ramifications of theme; its solution is effected by a series of reversals resulting from the logical investigation of a plausibly motivated sequence of events, an investigation that generates suspense in its continually delayed resolution and heightens that suspense through the evocation of imminent violence. This takes place in a fictional world vividly rendered through a technique that imbues object and landscape, behavior and gesture with the attitudes and concerns alive in the culture, thus capturing the spirit of a time and place. The merging of action, character, and setting raises significant human issues, which the novel carefully explores. And all this is presented in a style at once serviceable and felicitous, precise and resonant, a style with which the reader immediately engages and through which the writer achieves some remarkable effects.

All these excellences do not, however, constitute the primary excellence of *The Doomsters*. For the major expectation that we bring to a realistic novel is that it will move us, that it will bring us into the lives of "characters for whose fate we are made to care."[2] We expect a novel to show us these characters in a pattern of action that both grows out of and defines their essential nature; we further expect this action to significantly imperil these characters, so that its

outcome is of real consequence. (Of course the threat to the characters need
not be, and in most fiction is not, mortal; more often what is placed in jeopardy are vital relationships, attitudes, or values.) Thus, the success of a novel
is determined not by the quality of the ideas it may contain or the methods
through which these ideas are developed but by the degree to which it presents a significantly moving human action. In these terms, *The Doomsters* is
an eminently successful fiction.

Characters in whom we recognize a shared humanity abound in *The
Doomsters*. Even those peripheral to the action are drawn with compassion.
Early in the novel, for example, we meet Mrs. Gley, Mildred Hallman's
blowsy and alcoholic mother, "a middle-aged woman going to seed, but not
entirely gone. There was something about the way she carried herself: old
beauty and grace controlling her flesh, like an unforgotten discipline."[3]
Macdonald carefully contrasts her gin-smeared dreams with those of the "unreal shadows" on television: "The screen became a window into a brightly
lighted place where life was being lived, where a beautiful actress couldn't
decide between career and children and had to settle for both. The actual
windows of the sitting-room were heavily blinded" (36). Surveying the woman's dilapidated living room, Archer concludes, "it was no wonder Mrs. Gley
preferred darkness and gin and television to the light of morning" (38).
When Archer and Mildred are leaving, Macdonald fixes Mrs. Gley in all her
pathetic petulance and sad alcoholic posturing: "Her mother followed her, a
clumsy ghost trailing yellowing draperies and the powerful odor of Sen-Sen.
Either her earlier drinks were catching up with her, or she had another bottle
upstairs. She made her final plea, or threat: 'I'm drinking, Mildred.'" When
her daughter responds only with a weary "I know, Mother" and goes out the
door, Mrs. Gley screams an accusation that Mildred doesn't care about her.
Then, as Archer says, "Mrs. Gley turned to me as I passed her in the doorway.
The light from the window over the door lent her face a rosy youthfulness.
She looked like a naughty girl who was trying to decide whether or not to
have a tantrum"(41).

This typifies Macdonald's treatment of all the characters in the novel, his
deft illustration of their essential humanity. (I am not suggesting that
Macdonald wishes us to "like" these characters; rather, he would have us understand them, see them with all their foolishness and egoism and evil impulses as fellow sufferers of the human condition.) Even those who function
primarily to impede Archer's investigation—Sheriff Duane Ostervelt and
his deputy, Carmichael—finally stand before us as people and not "agents
of plot."

Those from whom the suffering and death appear to emanate are similarly treated. Zinnie Hallman, whose adultery seems at the center of the moral chaos swirling with destructive intent about the Hallman family, we first see, with Archer, as "a nice machine . . . pseudo-Hollywood, probably empty, certainly expensive, and not new; but a nice machine" (50). Between Zinnie and Mildred, Archer observes "a barrier of hostility, like a charged fence" (49); yet in the presence of death, Zinnie "put her arm around Mildred and hugged her" as the two women are "sistered by shock" (68).

If we are made to care about all the characters, we are primarily concerned with those whose separate actions merge to form the novel's central action. But it is indeed their fates about which we are made to care. In *The Doomsters* the notion of fate, of some dark cosmological force directing human affairs, assumes thematic centrality. Repeatedly the Hallman family is referred to in Aeschylean terms; their ranch house takes on a metonymic function, and the novel traces the destruction of the House of Hallman. This destruction has biblical antecedents as well. Commenting on present events, the old nurse Mrs. Hutchinson observes, "There's a line from the Word keeps running through my head since all this trouble today. 'The fathers have eaten sour grapes, and the children's teeth are set on edge'" (167). While social worker Rose Parish suggests that the attitude is "right out of Freud," Archer believes that she is "putting the cart before the horse. The Old Testament words reverberated in my mind" (167). So they reverberate throughout the novel, emanating from a single source, which the old nurse also identifies. Speaking of the suicide of Carl Hallman's mother, Mrs. Hutchinson explains the woman who is the primary cause of the present misery and death: "She was always talking about those Doomsters of hers. She believed her life was ruled by evil fates, like, and they had killed all the love in the world the day she was born. It was true, in a way, I guess. Nobody did love her" (187).

Fate, love, and guilt—these are the themes that Macdonald explores in *The Doomsters*. The themes themselves, however, gain significance only through the fictional action that they inform. And at the center of this action are the three characters about whose fate we are made to care: Carl Hallman, Mildred Gley Hallman, and, curiously enough, Lew Archer.

The Case

The case Archer works in *The Doomsters* begins at dawn as he is awakened from a dream by a "very large young man in dungarees" (3). Carl Hallman's physical appearance and fixed gaze suggest to Archer that Carl "could be in a bad way" (3). Archer quickly learns that Carl is the younger son of a recently deceased state senator from a small agricultural town, that he was diagnosed manic-depressive and committed to the state hospital, and that he escaped from the institution the previous night with a man who had sent him to Archer for help. Feeding Carl, Archer listens to his accusation that he was confined against his will by his older brother, who now controls the family property, and that a Dr. Grantland is also somehow involved in the conspiracy. Conspiracy or no, Archer perceives that Carl Hallman needs professional help. His conversation is erratic, his sense of time disjointed, his psyche haunted by the death of his father: "there was a strangeness in him, stranger than fear, which might be one of guilt's chameleon forms" (5). At last Archer proposes that they return to the hospital, after which the detective will try to determine if there is substance to Carl's theories.

On the ride toward the institution, Archer constructs from Carl's rambling talk a picture of the Hallman family: of Carl's brother, Jerry, a nonpracticing attorney "prematurely old in his middle thirties" (14) and married to Zinnie, "a blonde divorcee of uncertain origin" (14); of their father, Jeremiah Hallman, who "had been a power in the county, to some extent in the state . . . a successful man who had failed to transmit the genes of success to his two sons" (13); of their mother, who died a few years before, about whom Carl refuses to speak; and of Mildred, Carl's wife, whom he married over the family's objections. Carl also speaks of his emotional breakdown while a student at Berkeley and of his subsequent depression—"The other people in the house were like gray ghosts around me, even Mildred, and I was the grayest ghost of all. Even the house was rotting away" (15). With "an evangelical light in his eye" he describes his plan to return part of the Hallman land to the Japanese-Americans who lost the property while interred during the war. An argument about this had contributed to his father's fatal heart attack. Nearing the hospital, Carl explains that he had originally held himself responsible for his father's death: "I thought I was a parricide. But now I don't know" (15); now he wants to learn the truth. Archer, nearly convinced that he is "listening to paranoid delusions" (19), attempts to pacify the now distraught young man, but the attempt backfires. Carl overpowers Archer, knocks him out, and escapes in his car.

Obviously expository, the first brief chapters also serve to introduce a troubled and troubling young man. This initial presentation of Carl Hallman is crucial to the effect of the narrative. Carl does not reappear until near the end, but most of the action involves Archer's attempt to find the young man, to save him from a group of vigilantes led by a brutish sheriff, and to discover the "truth" that Carl also seeks. In this search Archer also uncovers the truth *of* Carl Hallman, so that his fate increasingly becomes the object of Archer's, and thus the reader's, concern.

At the hospital Archer learns from a psychiatrist that Carl's emotional problems stemmed from his misplaced guilt over both his father's death and his mother's suicide; from the psychiatric social worker Rose Parish he learns that Carl had been making "wonderful strides" (31). Archer observes that Rose Parish, a woman with "the kind of hips that are meant for child-bearing and associated activities," (28) and "the emotional equipment to match her splendid physical equipment," (32) has obscured her professional view of Carl with feelings both maternal and romantic. Nevertheless, the testimony of Rose and the psychiatrist establish the notion of Carl's innocence. Archer soon becomes convinced of it, for each character of whom he approves also confirms the young man's probity and idealistic naiveté.

In the small valley town of Purissima, Archer begins to talk with Mildred Hallman when they learn that her husband has been seen with a gun at the Hallman ranch. On the drive there, Mildred insists that the whole affair is the result of "the well-known Hallman greed" and that "Carl is good. It's often the best people who crack up" (44). Near the ranch they are stopped by Sheriff Ostervelt, a lecherous old man "whose eyes held the confident vacancy that comes from the exercise of other people's power" (46); that the sheriff clearly has a yen for Mildred Hallman and is leading the hunt for her husband does not bode well for the missing man. Thus, Archer begins his own hunt for Carl, which brings him in contact with other characters and leads to his conviction that Carl's conspiracy theory has a basis in truth. Both Jerry and Zinnie Hallman contributed to the events that led to his father's death, and either may have engineered it. Also implicated are Dr. Grantland, who is having an affair with Zinnie, and Sheriff Ostervelt, who was for years a henchman for the elder Hallman and whose handling of the senator's death was professionally inept and perhaps criminal. When Jerry Hallman is found shot to death with the gun that Carl had been carrying, and when Zinnie is discovered knifed to death, Archer knows enough about the Hallmans to remain convinced, despite the "evidence," of Carl's innocence.

With the discovery of Jerry Hallman's body, the sheriff recruits townspeople for an all-out manhunt, which forms the backdrop for much of the action and allows Macdonald to explore the dynamics of a community terrorizing itself with rumor and fantasy. Through Archer's brief observations, the townspeople's comments, and the distant alarums and bravado of the posse, Macdonald captures both the guiltily erotic essence of bloodlust and the post-MacCarthy paranoia that hovered over small-town America life in the 1950s. At the same time, as the involvement of the sheriff becomes more apparent to Archer, the actions of the posse he heads become more ominous; as

Archer becomes more convinced of Carl Hallman's innocence, the mortal danger to the young man by rifle-toting citizens becomes more imminent.

Until they are killed, both Jerry and Zinnie Hallman fall under Archer's suspicion in the death of Senator Hallman. While Zinnie is still alive, however, Archer comes to focus on Dr. Grantland, especially when the suicide of Carl's mother, whom Grantland had treated, comes under question. Grantland, whose face unsettles Archer by its ability to change "rapidly and radically" (61), had gone "through the college of hard knocks as well as medical school . . . when his patients couldn't pay him he went right on caring for them" (185). This until "the big change in him started up about three years ago" (185). Alicia Hallman died three years before. Gradually Archer discerns that her death, not her husband's, holds the key to the case. Her gun, with which Jerry was killed, becomes the pea in a shell game that Archer must solve; he finally locates it under Grantland's hand. Archer's suspicion edges towards certainty when he discovers that Zinnie was killed in Grantland's bed, and it solidifies after the doctor knocks him out, sets his own house on fire, and leaves Archer to die in the flames. Escaping the fire, Archer follows Grantland to Mildred Hallman's house, arriving just as Grantland puts several bullets into Carl Hallman.

"Perhaps in his central darkness Grantland yearned for death" Archer muses (208). In any event, the doctor ignores the warning of Sheriff Ostervelt and tries to run. Ostervelt fires, and Grantland, Archer assumes, "was dead before he struck the road" (209). Then, in one of the sudden humanizing gestures typical of Macdonald's fiction, the sheriff speaks: "I still don't like to kill a man. It's too damn easy to wipe one out and too damn hard to grow one" (209). Archer responds only to himself. "I liked the sheriff better for saying that, though I didn't let it run away with me" (209).

Carl Hallman, innocent of the murders of his father and mother, his brother and sister-in-law, is seriously wounded, but, as Archer observes, "Carl was a durable boy; he was still breathing when they carried him out" (211). Outside, "the street was filling up with people now. Rifles glinted among them, but there was no real menace in the crowd" (211). Less than twenty-four hours after Carl Hallman knocked on Archer's garage door, the case is over.

Except, of course, that it isn't.

The Story

The case that Archer investigates revolves around the question of the guilt or innocence of Carl Hallman. But the story the novel tells concerns not Carl but Mildred Hallman, "a human being with more grief on her young mind than it was able to bear" (220). Hers is a story of loss and guilt, deprivation and ambition, deceit and love, a story that traces a fate perhaps controlled by the cosmic agents of which Thomas Hardy wrote in the poem that Alicia Hallman loved to quote: "Sleep the long sleep: / The Doomsters heap / Travails and teens around us here." . . . Mildred's mother-in-law had explicated the poem for her, explicating Mildred's life at the same time: "She said it was written to an unborn child. Teens meant heartaches and troubles, and that's all any child had to look forward to in this life. The Doomsters saw to that. She talked about those Doomsters of hers as if they really existed. We were sitting looking out over the sea, and I almost thought I could see them walking up out of the black water and looming across the stars. Monsters with human faces" (225–26).

Mildred Gley Hallman is the most sympathetically drawn character in *The Doomsters*. Much of that sympathy, however, derives from Lew Archer's attraction to her. He is immediately caught by her youthful beauty—"She was young and small, with a fine small head . . . she had on a dark business suit which her body filled the way grapes fill their skins" (37)—by her intense gaze "almost tangible on my face" (38), and by his sense that "she was the one who had suffered most in the family trouble" (38). Yet Archer recognizes that his response to the young woman arises from conflicting impulses, with which he will struggle throughout the novel: "It started out as paternal sympathy but rapidly degenerated, if I let it. And Mildred had a husband" (42). Often he vacillates between the parental and the erotic, and sometimes he experiences these together, but always he colors his perception of Mildred Hallman in the hues of his emotion.

What Archer has the reader see is a young woman admirably if not always successfully attempting to cope with the travail by which she is beset. The demands of her mother, the snobbery of the Hallman family, the gross sexual overtures of Sheriff Ostervelt, her fierce loyalty to her husband, her frantic efforts to find and help him—all contribute to the portrait of a woman whose "loss was the worst. It had been going on for a long time, and was continuing" (70). Her struggle against the plague of events reveals a humanity so large as to subsume her sexuality; as Archer puts it, "She had something more provocative than sex: the intense grave innocence of a serious child, and a loneliness that made her seem vulnerable" (90).

Part of Archer's concern for Mildred is her inability to endure all that is being "heaped" upon her. At the Hallman ranch Mildred tries to show the deputy where she saw Carl: "She turned and started towards the open gate, moving with a kind of dogged gallantry. It wasn't quite enough to hold her up. Suddenly she went to her knees and crumpled sideways on the lawn, a small dark-suited figure with spilled brown hair" (64). Later, and more seriously, she reacts to Archer's comforting gesture by leaping from his car: "The situation went to pieces, and came together in the rigid formal clarity of a photographed explosion. Mildred was on the pavement, walking head down in the truck's bright path. It bore down on her as tall as a house, braying and squealing. I saw its driver's lantern-slide face high above the road, and Mildred in the road in front of the giant tires" (141). The truck manages to stop, and Mildred reacts "obliviously, like someone alone in black space" (141).

Occasionally, under the force of stress Mildred turns sharply on one of the other characters. With Zinnie Hallman and the sheriff she can be suddenly, if understandably, savage, and Archer himself can provoke retorts. These outbursts have the effect of further humanizing her, distancing her from the sort of sexual idealization that Archer's emotions threaten to establish. At the same time they provide Macdonald the opportunity to delve deeper into his thematic concerns. Nowhere is this more apparent than in her confrontation with Rose Parish.

Hearing that Miss Parish and the sheriff are coming to her home, Mildred excuses herself for reasons the novel has validated: "They're people-eaters . . . people who live on other people's problems. . . . I've had enough bites taken out of me" (148). After getting rid of the sheriff, Rose Parish enters Mildred's home with an officious suspicion that reminds Archer of "a female operative in a spy movie" (153). Her comment on the social difference between the Hallman and the Gley families "irks" Archer (154), and her Freudian explanation of Carl's guilt he finds overly simple: "It was a tempting doctrine, that Carl's guilt was compounded of words and fantasies, the stuff of childhood nightmares. It promised to solve so many problems that I was suspicious of it" (156). Finally Archer sees in Rose "the doubts and fears that had kept her single and turned her love towards the sick" (159). To her admission of love for Carl Hallman, Archer does not respond, being "reluctant to encourage her intimacy" (159).

Macdonald's characterization of Rose Parish is both subtle and sharp. At once "too personal and too official" (159), she is well meaning and pretentious, loving and snobbish, concerned and patronizing; given to Freudian analyses of everyone around her, she seems blind to the conflicts within her own psyche that can lead her to fix her emotions on the disturbed husband of another woman. A woman who would comfort and heal, she is a jargonridden bureaucrat ignorant of her own motives, and Archer deliberately separates himself from her.

When Mildred appears, however, Archer's attitude toward both women slowly, subtly alters. He quickly realizes that "the two young women had crossed swords or needles before" (160). In this encounter, Rose does not fare well: "Like other forthright people, Miss Parish got very phony when she got phony at all" (160). Soon, "large and outwitted and rebuffed, Miss Parish sank into a chair. Its springs creaked satirically under her weight. She tried to look small" (161). But Mildred continues to attack, finally eliciting Archer's sympathy for her victim: "Miss Parish was being badly mauled. Although in a way she'd asked for it, I felt sorry for her" (16). At last, sotto voce, he tells Mildred to "lay off" (161).

The effect of these few pages is powerful. Under an attack she brought on herself, Rose Parish is stripped of her pretensions, but what is revealed is a woman who, despite her artificial personality and vast ignorance, is capable of a suffering that elicits Archer's sympathy. Mildred, on the other hand, in the civil savagery of her perhaps justifiable assault, reveals a darker side of herself, so that while she remains central to Archer's concern, his idealization of her becomes more difficult. Each woman becomes, simply, more human. The conflict between them becomes more arresting, its outcome more problematic.

Its outcome is also inevitable, as is the fate of Mildred Hallman. For the truth of Mildred's story has been there all along, in her sudden self-destructive gestures, in her occasional darkly dramatic remarks that do not quite jibe with reality, in the nightmarish aura of sexuality and suffering, vulnerability and guilt that surrounds her. But not until Archer sees her despairingly submit to the hands and mouth of Sheriff Ostervelt does he understand. It is too late for him to do anything for her, of course; it has always been too late. Mildred's story is over; "her voice was dead. . . . As her heels tapped up the stairs I thought of a blind person in a ruined house tapping up a staircase that ended in nothing" (217). All her story requires now is its telling. She tells it in the final chapters of the novel, which are among the most powerful and moving in the history of the American detective novel.

The story that Mildred tells Archer cannot be summarized without trivializing it. But its effect is evident in his response: "Mildred was as guilty as a girl could be, but she wasn't the only one. An alternating current of guilt ran between her and all of us involved with her. Grantland and Rica, Ostervelt, and me." Linking Mildred's fate to her alcoholic mother and deserter father as well, Archer concludes that "the current of guilt flowed in a closed circuit if you traced it far enough." Then, in a passage all of Macdonald's critics focus on, he assesses Alicia Hallman's "Doomsters": "If they didn't exist in the actual world they rose from the depths of every man's inner sea, gentle as night dreams, with the back-breaking force of tidal waves. Perhaps they existed in the sense that men and women were their own Doomsters, the secret authors of their own destruction. You had to be very careful what you dreamed" (238).

The irony structuring Mildred's ghastly tale is starkly and profoundly Aeschylean. Alicia Hallman, driven by her doomsters to destroy her unborn grandchild, in that very act transformed the mother of that unborn child into the agent of those same doomsters. Both victim and agent, Mildred carries out their awful and at the same time inevitable charge, destroying not only Alicia Hallman but most of her family, destroying the House of Hallman.

Finally, Mildred's story has been told. The mystery is solved. Except, of course, that it isn't.

The Mystery

Of his detective narrator Macdonald once observed, "It took him a while to develop into anything substantial. The real change in him, I think, occurred in *The Doomsters;* he became a man who was not so much trying to find the criminal as understand him."[4] In *The Doomsters* Macdonald involves his detective in the action to the degree that Archer and his past become a subject of the story he tells, a story that is finally told in the novel's concluding pages, as Archer walks "through the day in the past when this story should have begun for me, but didn't" (249).

As the novel opens, Archer learns that Carl Hallman had been sent to him by the patient with whom Hallman escaped. At the hospital Archer discovers that the patient was a heroin addict named Tom Rica. Archer's reaction is disappointed but, as it turns out, self-serving: "Tom had played his part in the post-war rebellion that turned so many boys against authority. But he had been one of the salvageable ones, I'd thought. I'd helped to get him probation after his first major conviction—car theft, as usual—taught him a little boxing and shooting, tried to teach him some of the other things a man should know. Well, at least he remembered my name" (28). Having explained to himself Rica's role in sending Carl Hallman to him, Archer forgets Rica and sets to work on the case.

Nearly a hundred pages later, however, Rica suddenly reappears, meeting clandestinely with Dr. Grantland, who is now the subject of Archer's suspicions. The detective is as puzzled by this unexpected connection as he is stunned by Rica's physical deterioration—"The face behind the wheel . . . could have belonged to that boy's grandfather" (121–22). Following Rica,

Archer again assesses their earlier relationship. "When he was eighteen and his unmaturing youth had begun to go rank, I'd tried to hold him straight, and even run some interference for him. An old cop had done it for me when I was a kid. I couldn't do it for Tom" (122). This darker synopsis of the events, shaded by Archer's subtle but unacknowledged guilt, suggests an identification with and sense of responsibility for the younger man. In Tom, Archer had seen his youthful self; the young Archer had been saved, but the adult Archer had failed to save Rica. Then the recognition of his inadequacy in this relationship prompts the recollection of another: "The memory of my failure was bitter and obscure, mixed with the ash-blonde memory of a woman I'd once been married to. I put both memories out of my mind" (122). But these partially perceived memories will not remain in the darkness of deliberate forgetfulness. Tom Rica will not let them.

Archer follows Rica to a roadside brothel, where he tries to get Rica to tell him what he knows of the case. The young man responds with bitter sarcasm, calling Archer "old buddy" and "the do-gooder"; the conversation grows more heated when Archer tries to prevent Rica from shooting up, and Rica explodes into vilification, accusing Archer of hypocrisy: "You spout the old uplift line, but I never seen a one of you that believed it for himself. While you're telling other people how to live, you're double-timing your wife and running after skirts, drinking like a goddamn fish and chasing any dirty nickel you can see" (131).

The outburst silences Archer: "There was enough truth in what he said to tie my tongue for a minute. The obscure pain of memory came back. It centered in an image in my mind: the face of the woman I had lost. I blotted the image out, telling myself that that was years ago. The important things had happened years ago" (131–32). Again he turns away from the memories, from his past; again he refuses to confront the truth about himself that these "important things" would tell. But of course these things are still happening, still exerting their influence over him, still controlling his life. As the characters he observes are caught in the grip of their past, so is Archer the observer. His double failure with Tom Rica and his ex-wife Sue is the ground in which is rooted Archer's ambivalence toward Mildred Hallman. His emotional responses to the young woman careen between the paternal and the erotic, precisely those involved in his relationships with Tom and Sue. His failures in both instances finally paralyze him. He can act as neither parent nor lover with Mildred because he can not act confidently as either. Lew Archer is a prisoner of his own past, driven by his own Doomsters.

When Archer leaves the brothel, Tom Rica again vanishes from the action, only to reappear later at the end of a bloody trail on the sidewalk before Dr. Grantland's office. While Rose Parish comforts the young man, Archer calls for an ambulance. They do not meet again until the final chapter, when the case is over and Mildred's story is told. Except, of course, that the case is not over and the story not told. They cannot be, for they, along with Lew Archer's past, are all one.

The final chapter of *The Doomsters* is set in the local hospital, where Mildred is under both police guard and sedatives, Carl is still under anaesthesia from the operation to repair his wounds, and Tom is resting from his night of walking through heroin withdrawal. As Archer talks to Rose Parish, who has spent the night walking with Tom, he observes the change in her: "The night had left bruises around her eyes, which somehow improved her looks" (238). Surrounded by the wreckage of the Hallman family, Rose comes to an honest appraisal of herself, admitting her jealousy of Mildred, admitting too that she had suspected that Mildred suffered serious emotional problems but had said nothing about it. About the responsibilities for the destruction of the Hallman family, she says: "I've pretty well got over thinking in terms of good and bad. Those categories often do more harm than—well, good. We use them to torment ourselves, and hate ourselves because we can't live up to them. Before we know it, we're turning our hatred against other people, especially the unlucky ones, the weak ones who can't fight back. We think we have to punish somebody for the human mess we're in, so we single out scapegoats and call them evil. And Christian love and virtue go down the drain" (241).

Archer agrees, but, under the sway of those "categories," he finds himself thinking about Rica, finds himself again challenged by the memories he had blotted out: "I vaguely remembered a time in between, when hope and despair had been fighting for him, and he'd come to me for help. The rest of it was veiled in an old alcoholic haze, but I knew it was ugly" (241). So ugly is it, in fact, that Archer denies that his earlier relationship with Tom was of significance to the young man, denies that he knew that Rica had looked to him for help. Denies it only immediately to confess to himself, "I was lying. I knew. You always know" (242). Talking with Rica later, Archer listens to the young man's own horror story and to his accusations, watches as Rica "bared his arms as if the marks of the needle were battle scars; which I had inflicted on him" (245). The alcoholic haze shrouding his memory begins to lift; what he sees leaves him "a little nauseated" (245). Yet he still does not see it whole.

Tom Rica's final revelation, however, concerns neither himself nor Archer. Rather it is the truth about Alicia Hallman's death, a truth that gives the events of the action a kaleidoscopic shift and colors the entire case with tragic irony. Mildred Hallman did not kill her mother-in-law. Mrs. Hallman was killed by Dr. Grantland, while Rica watched. The irony compounds. It was Mrs. Hallman's murder that Rica had come to talk to Archer about three years before, when Archer refused to listen. Now, after three more murders—murders Mildred need not have committed, murders Archer might very well have prevented—Archer acknowledges his culpability, drags into the light of consciousness the mysteries of love and grief and guilt that haunt him, and tells his own story.

After a failed attempt to reconcile with Sue and an alcoholic lunch, Archer, locked into a fantasy of self-aggrandizement and sexual adventure, had made a date with a young blonde. Rica's unexpected arrival served to bring the junkie's street world into the office where the blonde might see it. More important, it brought in the real Lew Archer, the self and the life he would deny: "I'd been a street boy in my time, gang-fighter, thief, pool-room lawyer. It was a fact I didn't like to remember. It didn't fit in with the slick polaroid picture I had of myself as the rising young man of mystery who frequented beach clubs in the company of starlets" (250). Archer had hustled Tom Rica out of his office and life.

Facing himself three years and three murders too late, Archer can only conclude, "We were all guilty" (250), and resolve to abandon his dreams "where ash-blond ghosts were twittering" (251). But he cannot do so, for the dreams exist in the past, and the past is the present. Just over twenty-four hours before, in the novel's first sentences, Archer had awakened from a dream "about a hairless ape who lived in a cage by himself. His trouble was that people were always trying to get in" (3). Now that same hairless ape, the private detective Lew Archer, consciously attempts to free himself of his dreams, his past. For one brief moment he succeeds. "For once in my life I had nothing and wanted nothing." But only for a moment: "Then the thought of Sue fell through me like a feather in a vacuum. My mind picked it up and ran with it and took flight. I wondered where she was, what she was doing, whether she'd aged much as she lay in ambush in time, or changed the color of her bright head" (251).

Critics of Macdonald's work largely ignore *The Doomsters*. This results from the critical attitude that his significant achievement rests in the novels that begin with *The Galton Case*, novels deemed "quintessentially Macdonald" in subject and structure. Most critics mention the seventh Archer novel only to cite details of the detective's biography, and assessments of it are as superficial as they are rare. Jerry Speir, however, has recently admitted, "I still marvel at the construction of *The Doomsters*,"[5] and so might all readers, for it is an intricate narrative structure that skillfully plays on the reader's emotions as it propels him toward successive encounters with the darker realities of human existence. *The Doomsters* is a powerful novel, beautifully made.

Chapter Six
The Legend

Macdonald considered *The Galton Case* the work in which he first managed to transform his own experiences in such a way that the novel "broke free of my actual life and my rather murky feelings, into the clearer and more ordered world where fiction lays out its concentrated, terrifying version of the truth" (*SP*, 31). In it he also fixed the central themes and the pattern of action for the works to follow. The novels from *The Galton Case* through *The Blue Hammer* imaginatively render into mostly successful fictions the "crimes" of John and Anne Millar and the trauma of the young Kenneth Millar, as well as the perceived crimes of the adult Kenneth Millar and the suffering of his own child. Macdonald's last eleven novels represent his attempt to understand his past and his present, and this attempt comprises what he described as the "legend" of his life.

No one writing in the American detective novel has produced a body of work equal in either volume or overall quality to that of Macdonald's mature novels. Not that they are of equal value; several are less successful than the obvious triumphs. Generally in accord about which of the books are superior efforts, critics disagree about which of these is his best. Finally, however, their judgments seem rooted in personal taste. This is perhaps as it must be, for among the best of these novels there is really little upon which to base such choices. They are all excellent.

The Galton Case

Macdonald several times cited *The Galton Case* (1959) as his own favorite among the Archer novels, and his critics have been unanimous in their high regard for it. But while it may be his "most deeply felt" novel to date, as the flap blurb asserts, it is not his "most brilliantly plotted work."[1] As a detective novel, in fact, it is nearly transparent, its mystery not especially mysterious and its solution fairly obvious. That it nevertheless compels the reader's attention is testimony to the author's narrative skill, which is such that the novel works in spite of itself. On the other hand, the novel is crucial to Macdonald's career, the pivotal book in his oeuvre. A thematic fanfare, *The*

Galton Case trumpets the arrival into his fiction of those human dilemmas that would occupy him for the rest of his career. From this point on, the Archer novels may be identified as easily by their central psychosocial issues as by their narrator, for these issues constitute Macdonald's unique subject or donnée, which remains constant throughout his later work.

Although it tries to be a detective novel, *The Galton Case* is, as Edward Margolies observes, "a kind of bourgeois fairy tale."[2] The story, as pieced together by both Lew Archer and John Galton himself, follows a classic pattern of youthful fantasy. Through a childhood of crushing poverty and physical abuse, the boy Theo Fredericks clings to his mother's assertion that he is really a prince. "She said that I was a king's son, and we used to live in a palace in the sun. But the young king died and the bogey-man stole us away to the caves of ice where nothing was nice. She made a sort of rhyme of it. And she showed me a gold ring with a little red stone set in it that the king had left her for a remembrance."[3] When he is older, he learns from an evil stranger, Pete Culligan, that his putative father Frederick Nelson had murdered his real father, to which information he responds by attacking the "bogey-man" father and leaving him for dead as he flees with the evil stranger. The two are separated, the boy is taken in by a good stranger, Gabe Lindsay, becomes John Lindsay and learns the magical secrets—acting, in this case—that will provide him entry to the castle that, although he doesn't know it, is rightly his. Another stranger, Gordon Sable, appears with a scheme to place the young man in control of the castle, and Theo Fredericks/John Lindsay assumes the identity of John Brown, son of the missing heir to the huge fortune of the Galton family. The young man gains entry to the castle, then must flee it, but now in the company of a beautiful princess who loves him. Finally, with the help of the talismanic ring, the truth is revealed and the young man ends up in the castle with the princess at his side.

Overlaid on this fairy tale, of course, is the detective story. As a detective story, however, it doesn't really work, for the reader perceives early on the form of the underlying fable. So while Archer spends much of the novel sorting through the various twists and complexities of plot and motivation that Macdonald has set up for him, the reader already knows where the detective will end up.

The novel begins as a missing person case, which Archer takes on despite his conviction that "it's a waste of time and money" (25). Hired to locate Anthony Galton, scion of an immensely wealthy Santa Teresa family who has been missing for over twenty years, Archer swiftly confirms that the man has long been dead; at the same time he encounters a young man claiming to be the dead man's son. During the remainder of the novel, Archer works to establish the true identity of the young man. Vacillating between his suspicion that John Brown is a talented impostor and the "moral bet" he has made with himself that "John Brown was telling the truth. John Galton, that is" (130), Archer sorts through murders old and new, discovers the conspiracy behind a series of coincidences he cannot accept, explains a tangential connection between the case and some Nevada mobsters, and works through a set of reversals so that both he and John Brown simultaneously arrive at the truth: in posing as John Galton, John Brown in fact was impersonating himself.

Which comes as no surprise to the reader. For one thing, the clues that Macdonald has scattered about—especially those involving names—are fairly obvious. More important, the moral and emotional burden of the novel requires the conclusion. Repeatedly, those secondary characters of whom we are made to approve and trust testify to the essential moral probity of the young man. The logic of the action admits only two possibilities: John Brown is or is not who he says he is. Because he is good, he must be John Galton. Any other resolution would violate the emotional logic of the narrative.

Clearly Macdonald did not intend that the reader anticipate the explanation of the "mystery." In his discussion of the problems he had writing the book, however, he suggested the reason it happens: "Detective novels differ from some other kinds of novel, in having a rather hard structure built in logical coherence. But the structure fails to satisfy the mind, writer's or reader's, unless the logic of imagination, tempered by feelings and rooted in the unconscious, is tied to it, often subverting it" (*SP*, 57). Simply, Macdonald's own deep feelings about the character he called "the boy impostor" (*SP*, 58) subvert the logical structure of the novel in which the boy and his plight serve as the emotional center.

Actually, the structure of the novel is not all that logical to begin with. Before he can set out on his search for Anthony Galton, Archer is drawn into a murder case when Peter Culligan, the quite unservile houseman of Mrs. Galton's attorney Gordon Sable, is knifed to death and Archer's car is stolen by the obvious murder suspect. Almost immediately the detective suspects a connection between the murder and Anthony Galton's disappearance, for he distrusts the apparent coincidence of the events. Coincidence, however, plays a large part in the novel. Indeed, only through a sophisticated authorial legerdemain does Macdonald manage to distract the reader's attention from several of them.

"I hate coincidences," Archer muses. "Aboard the plane, I spent a fruitless hour trying to work out possible connections between Maria Galton's loss of her son and Peter Culligan's loss of life." Then he has a "delayed gestalt" (49), and works out the connection between a letter to Culligan from his ex-wife hinting at a mysterious event at "L. Bay" and the poem "Luna Bay" written by Anthony Galton under the pseudonym John Brown. By focusing attention on minor coincidences, Macdonald directs the reader away from those larger ones that allow his detective to possess these clues and involve him with Culligan's apparent killer. Beyond that, while later Archer observes that Culligan's "life ran through the case like a dirty piece of cord" (238), the man's involvement in the present action results from a coincidence of such magnitude as to seriously threaten the logic of the narrative in itself.

Despite its problems, the structure of *The Galton Case* is one of Macdonald's more interesting. As the plot develops it also, and quite genuinely, thickens. The "mystery" becomes more complex, if not more mysterious, while the action takes on meanings that accrue from Lew Archer's ingenuous observations. In the novel's first paragraph, for example, Archer jocularly describes his elevator ride to Gordon Sable's law offices as creating "the impression that after years of struggle you were rising effortlessly to your natural level, one of the chosen" (3); he quickly discovers, however, through the attitude of Sable's secretary, that "I wasn't one of the chosen after all" (3). This amusing little bit of business, as well as his sitting in a Harvard chair and feeling, when he rises, that "it was like being expelled" (3) actually shimmer with significance. As the narrative gradually makes clear, the story revolves around the notion of "natural levels" and the questions of who is "chosen" and how, of acceptance and expulsion.

The story also focuses on the question of identity—Macdonald considered titling the novel "A Matter of Identity." The central question of the novel is directed at young John Brown, of course, but it applies to most of the other characters as well, for few are what they seem, or in some cases believe themselves, to be. Of Maria Galton, the aged and ill widow who at once wishes to reconcile with her long-departed son and at the same time cannot quite forgive him, Archer says, "I suspected that she'd been playing tricks with her emotions for a long time, until none of them was quite valid" (20). Mrs. Galton's companion Cassie Hildreth is a "woman with a girl's body" (12), while Gordon Sable is a man in whom "the contrast of his tanned face with his wavy white hair somehow supported an illusion of youth" (3). San Francisco poet Chad Bolling, whom Archer finds reciting poetry to jazz in a beatnik bar (Archer's account of the reading is perhaps the funniest passage in Macdonald's fiction) is another character of uncertain identity—"Like other performers, he had a public face and a private one. Each of them was slightly phony, but the private face suited him better" (63). All of these uncertainties and illusions suggest the ultimate question of identity raised by the novel: Who, really, was Anthony Galton?

Talking with Mrs. Galton, her physician Dr. Howell, and Cassie Hildreth, Archer gets assessments of Anthony Galton that range from Howell's assertion that Galton was a biological and sociological "sport" whose primary excellences lay in "boozing and fornicating" (16) to Cassie's lovelorn description of a radical idealist who "was practicing Rimbaud's theory of the violation of the senses" (30) but who really wanted to do for the poor "what John Brown did for the slaves—in the spiritual sense, of course" (32). In the photographs he studies, however, Archer senses that even before the man disappeared there was something missing in him, and that "the missing feature was character or personality, the meaning that should have held the features together" (28). Throughout the novel Archer gets other views of Anthony Galton, but the true identity of the man remains a mystery, the unknowable primary source from which issues the suffering and injustice.

The nature and extent of this injustice Macdonald underscores by placing the action against a vividly rendered socioeconomic backdrop. The novel begins amid the old affluence of Santa Teresa, "an old and settled city, as such things go in California. Its buildings seemed to belong to the hills, to lean with some security on the past" (11). From the Galton estate, in a part of the city in which "massive traditional houses stood far back from the street behind masonry walls or topiary hedges" (11) and where lawns are mowed by "serfs," the action descends to its conclusion in a red boarding house on the edge of the river in Pitt, Ontario, in "a dreadful neighborhood, filthy children of all colors playing in the mud, and slatternly women screaming at them . . . where some men in their undershirts were sitting on the front steps passing around a wine jug" (190). In contrast to Mrs. Galton's neighborhood, the Arroyo Park section in which Gordon Sable has a "living machine, so new it hardly existed" is an "economic battleground where managers and professional people matched wits and income" (11). Lower are Marian Culligan Matheson's home in a junior-executive residential section where "flowers bloomed competitively in the yards" (100); the Marvista development in which "the houses were painted different colors, which only seemed to emphasize their sameness" (67); the weary San Francisco hotels; the workingman's boardinghouse that "hinted at a long history of decline" (124). As the neighborhoods vary, so do the inhabitants, from glossy manikins to human wreckage. Archer's impressionistic rendering of the world through which he passes colors it all with emotional and moral valuation, so that it is a matter of some urgency for the reader that the characters end up occupying those parts of the world that they deserve.

The Galton Case, then, is something of an anomaly. As a detective novel designed to allow the reader to accompany the detective as he investigates and solves a mystery, it doesn't really work, for the reader responds to the emotional logic of the action and intuits the solution long before the detective discovers it. The reader knows that the pauper is the prince and that he will receive the rewards and recognition rightly his due. Nevertheless, the reader remains fully engaged in the action, largely because Macdonald manages to render the socioeconomic significance of the restoration of John Brown to his proper position in such a way that it takes on moral significance.

Macdonald's comments on another early title of the book specify the nature of that significance. "'The Castle and the Poorhouse,' old-fashioned and melodramatic as the phrase is, accurately reflects the vision of the world which my adult imagination inherited from my childhood. It was a world profoundly divided, between the rich and the poor, the upright and the downcast, the sheep and the goats. We goats knew the moral pain inflicted not so much by poverty as by the doctrine, still current, that poverty is always deserved" (*SP*, 51). Poverty is evil, the novel says, and thus the good person must, if there is justice in the world, be able to live free of it. This justice determines all in *The Galton Case*, for it is justice for its characters and, vicariously, for its author.

Variations on a Theme

In the novels of the early and mid 1960s, Macdonald reworked the basic themes of *The Galton Case*—questions of identity and paternity, patterns of exile and return, realities of youthful suffering. If uneven in quality, these works—with one exception—succeed at a level of aesthetic and emotional coherence well above that of most efforts in the genre. And if they reveal a certain sameness of theme and characterization, they also demonstrate a subtle reimagining of material; they develop rather than repeat the insights, and deepen the mysteries of the fiction that precedes them.

Part of this development results from the gradual change in Lew Archer. Through these novels the detective ages, not so much chronologically as emotionally. While still physically adept and prone to occasional eruptions of anger, he less frequently engages in violence. Archer softens through these stories; the sharp edge of his personality dulls, the flaring heat at his core banks into coals. Yet he remains intensely involved in his cases, for despite his few attempts to make a human connection outside his work, these cases remain his primary bond with the human community.

The one case Lew Archer does not participate in is that of *The Ferguson Affair* (1961). The last novel Macdonald was to write without his detective as narrator, it is also a flat and unengaging work, thematically diffuse and finally not quite credible. A story of fathers and daughters, husbands and wives, and the psychological tension and confusion of those playing dual roles, the novel obscures most of what it attempts to clarify. The question around which the action revolves is whether Colonel Ian Ferguson has married his daughter; the question most puzzling to the reader, however, is why the movie starlet Holly May would marry Ferguson in the first place. The narrator, attorney Bill Gunnarson, is so distracted by his pregnant wife that he forgets to ask. Although it has many good things in it, *The Ferguson Affair* is finally an uninspired performance by a writer who had done and would do much better work.

Macdonald's next novel, *The Wycherly Woman* (1962), involves Archer in a "lost girl" case, which turns out to be another investigation into paternity and identity. The success of the novel hinges on the reader's willingness to accept the proposition that a twenty-one-year-old girl could without detection impersonate her forty-year-old mother, which Bruccoli delicately described as "an unlikely twist."[4] This proposition granted, however, the novel is marvelously moving.

In the character of Phoebe Wycherly, Macdonald created his most completely and compellingly realized version of the troubled young woman who haunts his fiction. The power of this characterization results from the narrative structure, for neither Archer nor the reader meets the real Phoebe until, long after the girl has been confirmed dead, she steps out from the personality she has assumed. Through most of the novel, Archer collects bits of information about the young woman, slowly piecing together a mosaic of her life and character; her appearance near the end of the action fuses that mosaic into a seamless and tragic portrait.

Archer is hired by Homer Wycherly, the ineffectual heir of an oil fortune and "a gentleman of the old school, as such things went in the sixties,"[5] whose daughter Phoebe disappeared from Boulder Beach College and was last seen with her mother, Wycherly's ex-wife Catherine. Wycherly describes Phoebe as "a complete innocent," but in the photo he shows Archer the detective sees "one of those sensitive girls who could grow up into beauty or into hard-faced spinsterhood. If she grew up at all" (8). At the college, Archer learns from Phoebe's babbling roommate that the missing girl was upset by her parents' divorce, and especially her mother's adultery, poison-pen letters about which precipitated the end of the marriage; he also learns that Phoebe was "*deep*" (26), and that she had "two or three personalities, one of them was a *poisonality*. She could be *black*" (26). Bobby Doncaster, the landlady's son and Phoebe's unannounced fiancé, confirms this and tells Archer that Phoebe had seen a Palo Alto psychiatrist the previous year. Later the girl's uncle, Carl

Trevor, describes Phoebe as "a fine deep girl who has had a hard growing up" (63), but again, in the photographs he's shown, Archer sees more: "The girl was almost beautiful in a poignant way of her own. Not beautiful enough, though; they never are" (63).

Unable to find the girl, Archer sets out to locate her mother, only to become involved with several characters on the scruffy edge of criminality. Almost immediately he stumbles onto a body. His pursuit of Catherine Wycherly entangles him in small-time real estate scams, but he traces her to a hotel in the Sacramento slums where "the night girls prowling the late streets, the furtive men in the doorways, looked sunk and lost forever in deep time" (81). Catherine Wycherly is gone, but Archer quickly locates her at an expensive motel. The woman he encounters is at once grotesque and pathetic: "Under the paint, her flesh seemed swollen and bruised, not just by violence, but by the padded blows of sorrow and shame" (92). After a bizarre and largely incoherent conversation in which, among other things, the woman tries to hire him to kill a man already dead, Archer leaves: "The horror in her was infecting me" (106). Outside her motel door he runs into a tire iron.

Soon Archer realizes that his involvement in the case has become personal: "I caught myself half-believing that Phoebe was my daughter. If she was dead, I would share Wycherly's loss" (118). His involvement deepens, and his hope is buoyed, when he talks to a cabbie who not only drove Phoebe and her mother the day the girl disappeared but also saw her some days later, standing on an overpass in pouring rain, "no raincoat, with her dress all wet and her hair striped down her face" (139). Tracing leads he got from the cabbie, Archer finds himself mixed up in another murder, but he escapes a lengthy interrogation by the authorities by invoking the name of Carl Trevor, who then informs him that Phoebe's car has been found by the sheriff in the seaside town of Medicine Stone. Trevor and Archer watch as a body is raised from the surf-smashed wreck: "The sea change she had undergone had aged her rapidly and horribly. She was beaten and bloated and ravaged" (192). Trevor identifies the body as that of his niece, then keels over from a heart attack.

Archer's response to the body is deeply felt: "A blur of tears stung my eyes, and a blur of anger" (192). He sets out to find Phoebe's killer, the immediate suspect being a young man who fits the description of Bobby Doncaster. But when he corners Bobby in a seedy Palo Alto motel, the young man finally tells the detective that the body pulled from the sea is that of Catherine Wycherly, and that Phoebe is in a nearby sanatorium under the care of the psychiatrist she had seen the year before. The doctor's diagnosis equivocates: "I think she hasn't decided herself which way she's going to go—towards reality, or towards illness" (244). In a long interview, however, the girl begins to move toward health; as Archer inquires into the murders and explains much of the case, Phoebe at last admits that her mother was killed by her father. Archer does a bit more checking, then confronts the killer, Phoebe's natural father Carl Trevor. Trevor writes a confession; in return Archer hands him a bottle containing a lethal number of digitalis pills.

The Wycherly Woman concludes on a hopeful note, at least insofar as it concerns Phoebe, whom we last see speaking of the child she carries; of the child's loyal father, Bobby Doncaster; and of the future the three of them can make. This note is not sounded in *The Zebra-Striped Hearse* (1962), Macdonald's next novel, which inverts the pattern of the preceding book. The troubled young woman in this story is also the killer; the father, out of guilt and despair but also out of love for the girl, kills himself in an attempt to make Archer believe that he committed the murders.

Jerry Spier suggests that *"The Zebra-Striped Hearse* is one of Macdonald's cleverest and most involved excursions into the Freudian 'family fantasy.'"[6] To label the subject Freudian, however, is to oversimplify and to some extent alter the focus of Macdonald's concern. What Archer finds himself enmeshed in is a psychosexual nightmare of stark suffering and elusive evil. While the text alludes to psychological theory, it also cites Greek drama, as Archer near the end of the action tells Isobel Blackwell: "The horrors will pass. Tragedy is like a sickness, and it passes. Even the horrors in the Greek plays are long since past."[7] Of course, Archer's own logic argues against this position, for he has earlier told Isobel, "The past is the key to the present" (230). In this story, the evil is traced back three generations, to the figure of Mark Blackwell's mother, who does not appear in the action: "Mark was her only son, and she really lavished herself on him, if 'lavish' is the word. 'Ravish' may be closer" (224). Yet if the past is the key to the present, the more distant past is the key to the behavior of Blackwell's mother. This past, of course, neither Archer nor the novel can investigate. Finally one can only treat it as the art critic Manny Meyer treats its spawn of evil: ignore it. Archer, however, regards this as unacceptable: Meyer "didn't believe in evil. His father had died in Buchenwald, and he didn't believe in evil" (112). The evil is real, Archer and the novel argue, but it is finally inexplicable, its initial impulse lost in the past, its present manifestations obscured by the muddle of human motive. Archer can deal only with its results: human suffering.

In his investigation of the mysteries of evil, guilt, and love, Archer receives assistance from a carefully patterned narrative structure. All the story lines, whose intersections Archer charts, arise in the Blackwell household. The characters who enact these stories occupy most of the niches in the lower to upper middle classes, ranging from a hopeful and curiously innocent chip-whore at Lake Tahoe to decadent expatriates drowning themselves in cheap-peso alcohol and ruined dreams in Mexico, from dreamy losers to self-righteous mediocrities. Each thematically fits neatly into balance with an-other, and through these characters the novel examines not merely the Blackwell family but the values of the society that produced it. These values are specific to the middle class; no character remotely resembles an under-world figure. In fact, Burke Damis/Bruce Campion, who for much of the novel appears to be a con man and killer, turns out to be as close to a hero as the novel allows.

The Damis/Campion transformation is but one of the character shifts in the novel. As Archer works through the case, fitting his observations to the perceptions and revelations of others, layers of duplicity and delusion fall away to leave characters in their naked if sometimes ambiguous reality. Harriet Blackwell, the rich girl who inherited not only a "fine big body . . . not meant for spinsterhood" (29) but also "the harsh bone that rose in a ridge above her eyes and made her not pretty" (22), at first seems the pa-thetic victim of her own passion and a gigolo's wiles. At the novel's end she is still a victim, but now tragically; she has killed everyone who seemed to threaten her envisioned happiness, but she has been unable to kill herself. Her father also changes, from a blustering and outraged fool to a weak-willed Humbert Humbert who marries to save himself from his fixation on young girls, to a guilt- and-grief-ridden parent who kills himself in an at-tempt to save his child.

All of this Macdonald lays out in patterns of dramatic action that reinforce meaning as they elucidate it. After interviews with first Isobel Blackwell and then her husband, Archer agrees to investigate the background of the painter Burke Damis, whom Blackwell's daughter Harriet intends to marry over her father's objection. Soon the detective understands Blackwell's concern, for in a beach house at Malibu he observes both Harriet's passion and Damis's re-sponse: "She leaned toward him, taller in her heels than he was, and kissed him on the mouth. He stood and absorbed her passion, his hands held away from her body. He was looking past her at me. His eyes were wide open and rather sad" (23). After breaking up a confrontation between Blackwell and Damis, who is leaving with Harriet, Archer sets out to learn what he can about the young painter. He first discovers that Damis entered and exited Mexico using the birth certificate of a dead man. Eventually he learns that Damis is really Bruce Campion, wanted for the murder of his wife. Tracking Campion and Harriet to a lodge at Lake Tahoe, he finds Harriet's bloodstained hat. Assuming that Campion has killed Harriet too, he pursues and captures him.

In eighteen swiftly moving chapters, Archer has apparently solved the case. Campion, however, denies all guilt. Archer then acknowledges that the authorities' version of events has some weaknesses, and he continues to investigate. The following thirteen chapters present a dazzling series of reversals, as Archer's suspicions of a character's guilt harden to near certainty until a casual remark or apparently irrelevant observation turns the case around and heads him in a different direction. He at last comes to a church in a small town in Mexico, where he finds Harriet Blackwell, who has out of love of both Damis and her father committed all the murders. She agrees to return with him. Leaving the church, Archer gives alms to a beggar. He has, he realizes, "nothing to give Harriet" (278).

In *The Zebra-Striped Hearse* Wilfred Sheed saw "that most reassuring of sights, a writer who seemed to know what he was doing. Macdonald had learned to finesse the conventions . . . he appeared to be easing out from the safe shallow waters where the hacks paddle in circles and into the gloomy depths of the Novel."[8] Macdonald had been out of the "shallows" for some time, of course, but in his tenth Archer novel he carefully and exactingly employed the conventions of the American detective novel to create a novel that took the genre where he had long attempted to get it—into the mainstream of American fiction.

Award Winners

Both *The Chill* and *The Far Side of the Dollar* received the accolades of Macdonald's peers, the first receiving the Silver Dagger Award of the British Crime Writers Association as the second-best novel of the year, the second the Golden Dagger Award. These novels may have been the best of those years; they are not, however, the best that Macdonald had written or would write. Both are intricate explorations of now-familiar thematic territory, but they are decidedly different in effect, and neither is without flaw.

The Chill (1964) is a plotting tour de force, a precise interweaving of three murder plots, which come to a sudden and totally unanticipated conclusion. Most of Macdonald's critics speak highly of the novel; Spier concludes that "it is one of his best books,"[9] and Wolfe recommends it for anyone wishing to read only one of the Archer novels.[10] Despite the masterful manipulation of its plot, however, the novel falls short of the achievement of some of Macdonald's earlier works, for it is finally all pattern and no center. The plot embroiders the predicament of two young lovers, Dolly and Alex Kincaid, and it is around their fate that the actions of past and present attempt to coalesce, but too many of the novel's events have little relevance to that fate. Beyond that, as T. R. Steiner has pointed out, the story of Dolly and Alex "usually is vapid."[11] Neither their characters nor their plight is of sufficient interest to engage our concern.

The response that Steiner describes has, I think, two causes. The plot is so complex that it requires special attention to follow. The patterns that Archer traces back thirty years and thousands of miles were created by characters long dead; such time and distance from the present action diminish the human significance of these patterns, so that Archer's piecing together the chain of causality seems motivated by curiosity or a sense of professionalism rather than by the imperatives arising from human suffering. At the same time, some of the characters involved are of more interest than Dolly and Alex, but the requirements of the plot force them to the periphery of our concern. For example, Steiner remarks on the vividness with which Helen Haggerty, the vital if slightly slatternly French teacher who is murdered early on in the action, remains in the memory. The same is true of her father, the broken-down ex-policeman whose coverup of a murder results in his daughter's murder thirty years later, as it is of Dolly Kincaid's father, whose character and plight are far more compelling than his daughter's.

Given these problems, it is remarkable that *The Chill* is as good as it is. The novel contains much that is memorable, and the final reversal is one of the most stunningly effective in the American detective novel. If it is less successful than some of Macdonald's other works as a significantly moving action, it is nevertheless clearly superior to anything anyone else in the genre was doing at the time. Still, like *Find a Victim,* if for quite different reasons, *The Chill* remains a collection of powerful fragments.

The same is true of *The Far Side of the Dollar* (1965), but again for different reasons. This novel stands as Macdonald's most vividly rendered vision of middle-class families ravaged by love and guilt, dreams and deceit and desire. A dark and troubling book, the novel records the suffering of parents and children, of lover and beloved, and transforms the neighborhoods of the American middle class in the 1960s into the landscape of hell. To do so, however, requires a plot patched together with coincidence, and a puzzling romantic relationship between Archer and an old flame that distracts the reader from the plot as much as it advances it.

The novel begins in hell, as Archer arrives at Laguna Perdida, a school for wayward adolescents, "a kind of prison which pretended not to be" (8). Archer's impressionistic account of the place is infused with Dickensian emotion. The adults range from the incompetent Dr. Sponti, who received his doctorate for a dissertation on "the kitchen logistics of a medium-sized boarding school" (16), to the supervisor Patch, so worn down by work for which he has no calling that he confuses authority with violence, to Mrs. Mallow, the alcoholic psychologist whose "life's meaning" Archer gets a glimpse of: "She cared for other people. Nobody cared for her" (17). Their charges are "boys of all ages from twelve to twenty, boys of all shapes and sizes, with only one thing in common: they marched like members of a defeated army. They reminded me of the very young soldiers we captured on the Rhine in the last stages of the last war" (8).

Archer is hired by Dr. Sponti to locate seventeen-year-old Tom Hillman, who escaped from the school a week after he'd been put there by his father. At Laguna Perdida the detective meets Ralph Hillman, "a large, impressive-looking man" whose face had the "patrician bony structure that doesn't necessarily imply brains or ability, or even decency, but that generally goes with money" (18). Tom, his father announces, has been kidnapped.

At the Hillman home, in "one of those rich developments whose inhabitants couldn't possibly have troubles" (24), Archer meets Hillman's wife Elaine, a small blonde woman in her forties of whom the detective observes "an aura of desolation hung about her, a sense of uselessness, as if she was in fact the faded doll she resembled" (26). From the Hillman's artificial yet anxiety-ridden conversation Archer gets "the impression that Tom was the center of the household, but a fairly unknown center, like a god they made sacrifices to and expected benefits from, and maybe punishments, too" (28). If Archer's observations of Laguna Perdida evoke Dickens, his account of the relationship of Elaine and Ralph Hillman prompts recollections of Sartre's *No Exit*. Husband and wife seem "actors improvising a tragedy before an audience of one" (27), a tragedy for which Ralph Hillman wears a "red savage mask" while his wife's face hangs "like a dead moon" (28), and which is set in a huge house in which the past is present "like an odor you couldn't quite place" (31). That past is, of course, the key to present difficulties, which cannot end until the truth of the past is acknowledged. As Archer comments halfway through the novel, "It gave me the queer feeling that time was repeating itself and would go on endlessly repeating itself, as it does in hell" (119).

Because the Hillmans refuse to discuss the real problems that led them to place their son in Laguna Perdida, Archer must search for a boy whom he neither knows nor understands. Beyond that, everything about the case seems wrong. The amount of ransom demanded by the kidnappers makes no real sense, creating in Archer's mind the possibility of the boy's collusion in the extortion. Through most of the action Archer confronts evidence suggesting that Tom Hillman is in league with the kidnappers. He cannot finally accept this evidence, however, largely because of the testimony of Tom's girlfriend, Stella Carlson.

Stella bears much of the emotional burden of the novel. Both Archer and the reader come to care about the fate of Tom Hillman only because of Stella's concern. But Archer's attitude toward the girl is informed by his own paternal impulses, so that he too embodies one of the novel's other themes—the relation of children and parents. As he talks with the girl, he has a sudden "evil image" of himself: "a heavy hunched figure seen from above in the act of tormenting a child who was already tormented. A sense went through me of the appalling ease with which the things you do in a good cause can slip over into the bad" (45). Stella's relations with her parents illustrate precisely this. Neither this nor the girl's apparently inveterate goodness, however, is sufficient to justify Archer's observation that Stella is "one of those youngsters who make you feel like apologizing for the world" (47). That the sentiment is deeply felt by both the detective and his creator is clear; that it is imposed upon the character rather than arising from the action is also clear.

From the inferno of middle-class domesticity, Archer makes his way into the hell of marginal criminality. Tom Hillman, he learns, has been seen with a blonde "old enough to be his mother" (59). Soon Archer literally stumbles over her body. Attempting to identify the woman, he shows pictures of her battered face to the denizens of the Hollywood Strip, without success: "The guys and dolls pursuing the rapid buck hated to be reminded of what was waiting on the far side of the dollar" (87). Finally Archer is led to an old flame, Susanna Drew, who identifies the woman as Carol Harley, her former roommate.

From this point Archer has twin concerns, for while he still searches for Tom Hillman, his interest in Susanna has been rekindled: "Something about her dark intensity bit into me as deep as memory" (96). Unfortunately, what that "something" is the reader never discovers. The Susanna Drew whom Archer describes is a woman of artificial emotion and brittle charm, so that when it becomes evident that she is somehow involved in the murderous events, the reader can only puzzle over Archer's distress. Bruccoli has reported that the relationship of Archer and Susanna was given a past only in the final draft of the manuscript, which suggests that Macdonald himself perceived the problems with it. Even with a past, however, the problems remain, for it is a relationship stated rather than dramatized, and its superficiality renders it incapable of carrying the emotional burden Macdonald places upon it. Archer would believe that it produces his own hell: "Now the case was taking hold of her skirt like the cogs of an automated machine that nobody knew how to stop. I have to admit that I wouldn't have stopped it even if I knew how. Which is the peculiar hell of being a pro" (165). If it is hell, it is one the reader cannot appreciate.

Following a course charted by clues, information, and intuition, Archer finally tracks down the truth of the dead woman, of her family, and of Tom Hillman. He journeys between two poles, a small town in Idaho and the Barcelona Hotel in Santa Monica. In Idaho he finds two families that complement the thematic significance of the Hillmans and Carlsons. Carol Brown Harley's mother and father, a small-town beauty whose fate has "defrauded" her and a high school coach with a face like "a late Roman general's, after a long series of defeats by barbarian hordes" (137), respond to Archer's inquiries with accusations and bickering. Wracked by the destruction of their dreams, the Browns can deal with neither their loss nor each other. By contrast, the Harleys are an old farm couple, he religion-crazed and given to invoking the Lord's wrath, she a woman in whom Archer sees "suffering half transformed into understanding" (131). The Harleys also bring Archer to thoughts of the inferno: "Just now it was easier for me to imagine a literal hell" (134).

In the Harley home, Archer and the novel locate the source of much of the evil that spreads through the lives of the other characters. Mr. Harley's religious mania and sadism have left their mark on people he never met as clearly as they left scars "like hieroglyphics recording history" (112) on the backs of his sons. But another source of evil is Otto Sipe, the ex-policeman, shakedown artist, and kidnapper who—much like Pete Culligan in *The Galton Case*—has exercised his malevolence on the action from beginning to end. Sipe's evil is one that Archer never does explain. But he places it and Sipe symbolically in context, for we never see the man except at the Barcelona Hotel.

Long closed, the Barcelona is "early Hollywood Byzantine, with stucco domes and minarets, and curved verandahs where famous faces of the silent days had sipped their bootleg rum" (99). Still fitted with the accoutrements and appointments of the past, the hotel is now a wreck housing only ghosts, dead dreams, and Otto Sipe. But everything important occurred at the Barcelona—Ralph Hillman's affair with Susanna Drew, his impregnation of Carol Brown Harley, the discovery of these affairs by Otto Sipe. Things continue to happen there; Tom Hillman hides in the hotel as he tries to learn the truth of his parentage, and Mike Harley and Otto Sipe die there, in a construction of dreams now "dead as Ninevah" (154).

Gradually Archer fits the past with the present, finds Tom, uncovers affairs long past, and identifies the killer—Elaine Hillman. Her plea for help in committing suicide rejected by Archer, she stabs herself to death with the needles with which she has been knitting, Madame LaFarge–like, throughout the novel. At the novel's conclusion, everything fits together. But not very satisfactorily.

At this point in his career, Macdonald was in no danger of writing a lifeless scene, and this book contains as much felt life as any of his fictions. Still, the elements of the novel fail to cohere. Major themes conflict with rather than complement each other, the characters about whose fate we should care are seen too briefly or are insufficiently dramatized to elicit real concern, and Archer himself seems uncertain what it all adds up to. There is about the novel, finally, an incompleteness, as if it were an early draft. The power of individual scenes distracts attention, on first reading, from some of the plot coincidences and thematic gaps, and a few of Archer's observations— "Generation after generation had to start from scratch and learn the world over again. It changed so rapidly that children couldn't learn from their parents or parents from their children. The generations were like alien tribes islanded in time" (141)—strike with such force that we forget that they are largely imposed on the action. But on closer reading, the problems appear.

With the Archer novels of the early and mid 1960s, Macdonald established himself as the foremost practitioner of the American detective novel. But he did not do this through his use of personal themes and concerns, however important they were to him. While it is obvious that his focus on family dynamics and their roots in the past identify his mature work, they do not account for its quality. That lies in his art. As Sheed pointed out, Macdonald had learned to "finesse" the conventions of the genre—to use them for his own purposes. He had also learned to use those devices and techniques more common to the "serious" novel, so that his "imagined actions" could be structured to create effects appropriate to his subjects and the "imagined retrospect" of Archer's narration could shape and lend significance to those actions. In these works, Macdonald demonstrated that he was not simply a fiction writer but a novelist. He also demonstrated that the American detective novel was "a convention or structure in which almost anything could be done."

Chapter Seven

Two Classics

Two of the three Archer novels that Macdonald wrote near the end of the 1960s are demonstrable "classics" in the popular sense of the word. While *The Instant Enemy* is a memorable if flawed work, both *Black Money* and *The Goodbye Look* stand in the highest rank of the American detective novel. Each is as good a novel as the genre has produced, and each illustrates the flexibility, strength, and precision of Macdonald's mature art. At the same time, although they differ significantly in structure and effect, the two novels have in common something of the ambience and art associated with classical literature. In their narrative economy and formal elegance, as well as their use of revelation and reversal, they suggest the emotional rhythms of Greek drama. For all the human horror at their centers, for all the passion and madness driving their characters, *Black Money* and *The Goodbye Look* work with moral and aesthetic inevitability, leaving the reader both with the satisfaction produced by the unraveling of a mystery and with that renewed and enlarged sense of his own moral and mortal existence that is the effect of significant art.

Art and Essence

Macdonald thought that his conception and use of Lew Archer as a Carrawayesque peripheral narrator was his major and distinctive contribution to the form he worked in, and that *The Galton Case* was the novel in which he turned that form into a vehicle for his own unique artistic purposes. Both of these claims are sufficiently true, but the novels of the late 1960s reveal an even more essential development in his art, one that discovered even greater aesthetic possibilities in the American detective novel.

Nearly any page of these three novels demonstrates the change in Macdonald's art. The prose is lean, the sentences short, the paragraphs brief. Archer, who in the foregoing novels had grown somewhat garrulous in both conversation and commentary, speaks now in a laconic voice more reminiscent of Hammett's Op than of Chandler's Marlowe. Less inclined to detailed description than to impressionistic summary, more apt to express observations and evaluations in hard images than in lyrical evocations, Archer's new voice creates new effects. For example, in *The Instant Enemy* he is knocked out, then returns to consciousness on a highway as a truck bears down on him, "honking repeatedly. Its brakes were shrieking, too, but it wasn't going to be able to stop before it got to me. I lay down and watched it blot out the stars. Then I could see the stars again, and feel the blood pounding all through my body."[1] The rhythms are Hammett's and Hemingway's rather than Chandler's and Fitzgerald's. But borne on these rhythms are Macdonald's own images, now largely refined of sentimental impurities.

The difference in Ross Macdonald's earlier and later style is illustrated by the following passages, the first from *The Wycherly Woman:* "Money flowed through the state capital like an alluvial river, and the Hacienda Inn was one of the places where the golden silt was deposited. It lay off the highway north of the city, sprawled on its golf course like a separate village. A Potemkin village, maybe, or the kind the French kings built near Versailles so they could play at being peasants on sunny afternoons" (91). A passage from *Black Money* is of similar purpose but quite different effect: "Montevista is a residential community adjacent to and symbiotic with the harbor city of Pacific Point. It has only one small shopping center, which calls itself the Village Square. Among its mock-rustic shops the Montevistans play at being simple villagers the way the courtiers of Versailles pretended to be peasants."[2]

This stylistic change alters other elements of the fiction. In this pared-down prose, images bear more of the thematic burden, many of them taking on symbolic qualities. The shift from image to symbol is sometimes subtle. In *The Goodbye Look,* for example, an obviously central symbol is the gold Florentine box whose theft brings Archer into the case; several times it is described in terms of the Pandora myth, and its opening unleashes crimes and chimeras confined for over twenty years. Less obvious are the symbolic implications of Archer's observation as he passes the courthouse: "In a cast stone bas-relief above the entrance, a big old Justice with bandaged eyes fumbled at her scales" (157). The image is saved from triteness by "bandaged" and "fumbled," both of which add thematic implications to the figure, so that it becomes the locus of multiple meanings. All this gives particular pertinence to Archer's famous remark, "I have a secret passion for mercy . . . but justice is what keeps happening to people" (127).

The change in the prose is not, however, the main difference of these later novels; it is simply the result of a new aesthetic, one resulting from Macdonald's increased distance from his material. In the earlier books Archer regularly comforted other characters, and his creator, with observations on the pointlessness of blame and accusation, on the transitoriness of even the most crippling guilt and enervating pain. The later novels are the work of a writer who, having to some extent accepted these consolations, has also accepted his characters. No longer compelled to probe characters in search of pain or guilt, Macdonald now allows them simply to be, to act, and to reveal that pain or guilt through those acts. The actions of these characters blend into the larger action of the novel, which becomes what Macdonald said his plots were intended to be, "a vehicle of meaning."

Just how these plots carry meaning can be appreciated, I think, if we view of plot, with R. S. Crane, as "a particular synthesis of particular materials of character, thought, and action . . . endowed necessarily . . . with a power to affect our opinions and emotions in a certain way."[3] Crane's formulation brings into consideration those narrative methods and devices we deem *spatial*—the paralleling, mirroring, or counterpointing of ideas, characters, scenes, or images—designed to affect our response. In his later novels Macdonald relies heavily on these devices to add meaning and to lead the reader to think and feel in specific ways. Often they point toward irony, and often that irony is tragic. To see, for example, that in *The Instant Enemy* Davey Spanner is killed by a man who would be the young man's friend is to see what the action shows us. To see that Davy's pursuit of his "real" father leads to his death at the hands of his "true" father, and that the deadly act results from that father's concern for his unborn "real" child is to see something akin to what we see with Oedipus, in all its fortuitousness and inevitability.

This results in a thematic elucidation far more complex than in the earlier fiction. In the later novels Macdonald breaks no new thematic ground; they too are about the relations between generations, the problematic nature of love and guilt, the question of evil. But their resolution is much less clear. The essential mysteries of these novels are never solved. They deepen, become even more mysterious. The cases end, but the mysteries remain.

Macdonald's constant thematic concerns, his relatively small cast of characters, and the similarities of the temporal structure of his plots have led some critics to complain of the "sameness" of these novels. Macdonald was aware of these complaints, but he felt the obligation neither to defend his methods nor to change them. Rather, as he reworked these themes, he more finely discriminated among the human meanings they yielded. His central subject, the object of his fictional inquiry, was inexhaustible, unresolvable. But he would not abandon it, for "it's all inside you . . . what you have to say. And you have to keep saying it over and over again, getting closer each time to what's true."[4]

Black Money

Macdonald's critics speak highly of *Black Money* (1966), and one insists that it is the best of the Archer series.[5] Certainly it is the most overtly "literary" of his novels. As nearly everyone has observed, the novel is the result of Macdonald's long meditation on the themes and patterns of action in the book he said he read annually, *The Great Gatsby. Black Money* is filled with references to Fitzgerald and his novel, and the case Archer takes on initially concerns the identity of a character whose life follows a Gatsbyesque pattern of early poverty, realization of idealistic dreams, and tragic destruction. But the story that Archer tells has beneath its surface a carefully composed pattern of characters, scenes, and incidents that create effects rarely found in detective fiction.

Archer is hired to determine the identity of a young man who calls himself Francis Martel and claims to be a member of an aristocratic French family and political refugee from the De Gaulle regime. Although Archer is genuinely puzzled by Martel—"I didn't know what to make of him" (31)—his investigation soon reveals that, far from being of noble French birth, Martel is Panamanian Felix Cervantes, a deck hand who several years before had jumped ship in California and who once worked as a bar boy at the Montevista Tennis Club, where much of the early action is set. Additional evidence, most of which Archer finds after Martel's death, proves that Martel/Cervantes was really Pedro Domingo, the grandson of a French engineer and a native Panamanian woman. Growing up in the slums of Panama City with a B-girl mother, Domingo opposed the grim reality of his life with a "geneological fantasy" (211) about descending from French aristocracy on one side and Sir Francis Drake on the other, and he dreamed that he would ascend to the pinnacle of French society. During his first stay in California, Domingo took college classes in French literature, impressing his instructor with his brilliance. He also became enamored at first sight and from afar, like Dante with Beatrice, of the lovely young student Ginny Fablon, even composing "sonnets about her and her ideal beauty" (213). The two never spoke, but Domingo's idealism nevertheless made her the embodiment of his romantic vision. Domingo left California with Las Vegas gambler Leo Spillman, who financed his education in England, after which the young man entered the Panamanian Foreign Service and used his diplomatic status to carry out of the country the "black money" that Spillman had skimmed from a Las Vegas casino. Then Domingo stole that money and returned to Montevista as Francis Martel, for the purpose of marrying Ginny.

Domingo succeeds in his quest, as he and Ginny marry shortly after the novel begins. But the realization of his idealistic dream leads to his destruction—a few days after the marriage he is shot to death. Unlike Gatsby's death, however, Domingo's does not result from the confrontation between his romantic ideal and the brutal reality of contemporary society; the agent of his death is a dream as idealistic as his own, that of Professor "Taps" Tappinger.

Tappinger also grew up in the slums, those of Chicago. After a stint in the service, he educated himself on the G.I. Bill and took a position in the French Department at the University of Illinois. "The rising young man in the department," Tappinger developed a relationship with a seventeen-year-old student; as another former student of Tappinger describes it, "the two of them had this Platonic thing going. They were like Adam and Eve before the Fall. Or Heloise and Abelard . . . then real life reared its ugly head" (216). The young woman, Bess, became pregnant, but despite the fact that she and Tappinger married, he was fired for "moral turpitude and sent to the boondocks" (216). His teaching load at Montevista State is so arduous that it prevents Tappinger from working on his book about "the luminous city . . . the world of spirit and intellect, the distillation of the great minds of past and present" (185). It does not prevent him from conducting a seven-year-long affair with Ginny Fablon.

The apex of this idealistic-erotic triangle, Ginny Fablon is an intelligent and lovely young woman whose past has fragmented her personality. The agent of this fragmentation was the father whom she idolized, who forced her to have an abortion, and who attempted to use her as payment for gambling debts. Unsuccessful in his pandering, Fablon seven years before had told his wife and daughter that he was going to kill himself; two days later his body was found in the sea. As his widow tells Archer, "God only knows what it's done to my daughter's emotional life" (102). Archer gets a clue to the state of the young woman's psyche when, after the murder of Martel, Ginny seems unable to recognize that her mother has also been murdered, and she begins to refer to her parents by their Christian names; Archer remarks, "I reminded myself that she wasn't a girl, but a woman with a brief tragic marriage already behind her. And what sounded like a long tragic childhood. Her voice had changed perceptibly, almost as though she had skipped from youth to middle age, when she began to call her father 'Roy'" (160).

But Archer's explanation is incomplete. Ginny's relationship with Tappinger has had an equally destructive effect on her emotional state. Beginning in idealism, the affair grew steadily more corrupt, culminating in a plan for Ginny to marry and then quickly divorce her rich young neighbor Peter Jamieson so that she and Tappinger can flee to Paris with the settlement money. When Martel arrived, he became the object of the plot. At the novel's end, when the extent of the corruption becomes clear, its source becomes problematic. Has Tappinger, whose gradual moral deterioration led him to three murders and suicide, corrupted Ginny, or has she corrupted him? The answer lies in the startling final image of the novel: "She was lying on the sitting room floor face to face with Tappinger, their profiles interlocking like complementary shapes cut from a single piece of metal" (238).

This fusion of complementary pairs into a single image suggests both the function and significance of the many pairs of characters and incidents in the novel. The pairing of Domingo and Tappinger is obvious and central, but there is hardly a character without a thematic doppelgänger. Archer himself has two: Harry Hendricks, a would-be detective and congenital loser (Hendricks once lost his wife in a crap game, which thematically parallels Roy Fablon's attempt to pay his gambling debts with his daughter); and the young policeman Ward Rassmusson, in whom Archer recognizes a version of his youthful self: "when I was a rookie on the Long Beach force, I had felt very much as he did. He was new to the harness, and I hoped it wouldn't cut too deep into his willing spirit" (124). This is not, of course, merely pairing and paralleling for the sake of an abstract pattern. The action of the novel reveals elements of character and thematic meaning; within the pattern, however, character shifts subtly, and meaning deepens.

Overlaid on this elaborate system of doubled characters and incidents is the narrative structure—a structure unlike anything we might normally expect to find in detective fiction. In the case that Archer narrates, he rarely comes into direct contact with the three characters whose interrelationships form the novel's central concern. Most of the novel describes Archer's conversations with secondary characters—close friends and relatives of Ginny and Tappinger, or those like Kitty Hendricks who function in a contrapuntal subplot—and a host of incidental characters such as hotel clerks, receptionists and bartenders, and members of the Tennis Club. These minor characters give Archer the information he needs to solve the case. At the same time, through their attitudes toward and remarks about the central characters and events, they comment on the significance of both, becoming in effect a chorus.

By distancing Archer and the reader from the main characters, Macdonald creates subtle effects. Domingo's death, for example, produces no strong emotional response, for the reader at that point knows little about him and has no intense concern for his fate. As the action proceeds, however, and Archer discovers more of the truth about the young man, his death takes on more emotional and thematic significance. At the same time, Domingo remains largely the "idea" of a character. The more we learn about the "reality" of the young Panamanian, the grander his romantic illusion becomes. His murder thus becomes the destruction of an ideal. The narrative presents Tappinger in the same way, but to quite different ends. As Domingo rises in our estimation, Tappinger sinks; as the young Panamanian's dream takes on the shape of a tragic destiny, the professor's is revealed as the last fantastic resort of the egoist.

This sort of narrative distancing is, of course, precisely the method Fitzgerald used to transform the "elegant young roughneck" who "just missed being absurd"[6] into the mythic figure of Jay Gatsby. Consequently, the Domingo we end up with is, like Gatsby, less a character than a symbol. But unlike Gatsby, Domingo does not achieve mythic stature, for the power of his romantic vision ebbs when placed next to Professor Tappinger's. Tappinger's and Domingo's dreams are similar in motivation and object, but as the ideal that Domingo pursues grows more quixotically impressive, that of the professor becomes corrupt, pathological, and murderous. "Tappinger was breaking up, had been breaking up when I first walked in on him" (231), Archer observes late in the novel, and such a disintegration is inevitable, for Tappinger's dream of life in Paris with Ginny, a life of intellectual eroticism in which "real life" does not "rear its ugly head," is as absurd as his notions of the "luminous city." In this context, Pedro's vision becomes as artificial as his geneology; as romantically appealing as Pedro's ideal may appear, it is finally of a piece with Tappinger's. They are not "good" and "bad" versions of the same dream but "complementary shapes" cut from the same piece of fantastic metal.

Highly wrought, tightly controlled, *Black Money* is a novel of subdued effects. It contains little physical action, little violence, little suspense. Neither Archer nor the reader comes into intense emotional contact with the characters. Except for Pedro Domingo, these characters are palpably real, but the narrative does not ask us to feel deeply for them. It asks, rather, that we see them as they are, in all their troubled humanity, and that we contemplate the nature of the human error that causes this trouble.

The Instant Enemy

There is nothing subdued or contemplative about Macdonald's next novel. Nearly as angry a book as the earlier *Blue City*, *The Instant Enemy* (1968) assaults the reader with a violence and horror as powerful as that which assault the two young characters who stand at its emotional center. Here Macdonald brings together the two characters who dominate his fiction—the angry young man searching for the truth of his past, and the disturbed young woman whose emotional turmoil results from the actions of the adults around her. The anger of the novel emanates, to a certain extent, from Davy Spanner, the self-described "instant enemy" of himself and everyone around him. But it comes as well from Lew Archer, as he discovers both the truth of Davy Spanner's life and the details of the emotional and physical brutalization of Sandy Sebastian, the young woman he is initially hired to find. From the beginning of the action, Archer continually encounters characters, events, and attitudes that induce his ire. Struggling to maintain his calm in the face of the delusionary folly and petty concerns of the people he meets, Archer can only seethe at their egoistic ignorance of the consequences of their attitudes and actions. *The Instant Enemy* is a bitter book, but the bitterness is eminently justified, as Archer's anger is a reasonable response to the destructive self-indulgence that rules most of the characters. Davy Spanner is an instant enemy of this society of artificial values and threadbare morality, but so is Lew Archer.

The novel opens on a pristinely peaceful note, as Archer crests a low pass in the Los Angeles hills: "For a minute or two, before the regular day set in, everything looked fresh and new and awesome as creation" (3). The "regular day" soon destroys that peace, however. In "an angular contemporary house cantilevered out over a slope" (3), Archer talks to Keith and Bernice Sebastian and agrees to look for their missing seventeen-year-old daughter, Sandy, who her father says is "running wild with a criminal" (6). The discussion makes it clear that the Sebastians are a family "cantilevered out over a slope" and that their grip on familial unity is precarious. Irritated by the bickering of husband and wife, Archer silently proclaims, "I was weary of the war of the generations, the charges and counter-charges, the escalations and negotiations, the endless talk across the bargaining table" (6). By the time he leaves, however, he has begun to sympathize both with Sandy Sebastian and the "criminal," nineteen-year-old Davy Spanner.

Archer finds the two young people quickly enough, at the Laurel Apartments where Davy works as a handyman for the owner-manager, Mrs. Laurel Smith, a woman who "sort of went with the red hibiscus" (20) in her garden. At Davy's apartment, the young man peers "out at the sunlight as if it had rejected him" (21). When Sandy comes to the door, "her body thrust itself forward and leaned on Davy's with the kind of heartbroken lewdness that only very young girls are capable of" (22). After a brief scuffle in which Archer gets "taken" (24), he stakes out the apartment building but loses Davy and Sandy when they leave. Driven by a sense of urgency compounded of his awareness of the violence in the boy and the volatility produced by his relationship with Sandy, Archer nevertheless maintains a sympathy for both. Thus his concern is personal as well as professional.

Tracing the young people, Archer uncovers what appears to be their plot to kidnap Stephen Hackett, a wealthy businessman and owner of the savings and loan company Keith Sebastian works for. Hackett, Archer observes, gives "the impression of wearing his money the way other men wear elevator shoes" (39). Archer also discovers a badly beaten and unconscious Laurel Smith, as well as a hidden microphone in her apartment. Soon he learns that an ex-sheriff named Fleisher has bugged her apartment and has also been asking questions about Davy Spanner, and he receives the news that Davy and Sandy have attacked a ranch employee, Lupe Rivera, with a tire iron and abducted Hackett. After talking with Hackett's mother, a woman with over fifty "years accumulated behind her youthful facade" who had earlier assessed Archer with "the arithmetical eye of an aging professional beauty: would I be viable in bed?" (48), Archer sets out in pursuit of the two young people and their captive.

At the same time, Archer has been piecing together the history of Davy Spanner. As he follows the trail, he also tracks Davy's life; his delving into the past becomes a descent into horror. From Henry Langston, a high school counselor who admits to a "terrible empathy" (83) with Davy, he learns that the boy had been found fifteen years before, a three-year-old who had spent a night beside the body of his father, who had fallen from a train and been decapitated by it. The father was never identified, and the son was placed in an orphanage, from which he was taken by a couple named Spanner. Mrs. Spanner would see their time together as "ten good years," but her husband, who lost his lay preachership in "the Holy Brethren of the Immaculate Conception" when Davy got into trouble with the law, remembers it otherwise: "Hardly a day went by that I didn't have to use the razor strap on him" (58). The trail also leads Archer back, through an elaborate set of relationships of which the ex-Sheriff Fleisher is the linchpin, to the Hackett household. A sordid story of greed, cupidity, and murder gradually unfolds, in which Davy is clearly a casualty. But as Archer gets closer to the truth, time and circumstance close in on the young man. Archer finds Stephen Hackett alive, but he finds Jack Fleisher dead, at Davy's hand. Evading the law, Davy finally surfaces at Henry Langston's home. In an act superficially justified by the situation but nevertheless complex and ambivalent in its true motivation, Langston kills him. Archer leaves, "stepping wide over the threshold where some of Davy's blood was turning brown in the sun that had rejected him now forever" (194).

Archer also uncovers the hideous crime at the root of Sandy Sebastian's emotional turmoil. The summer before she had been dosed with LSD and violated by Stephen Hackett and Lupe Rivera. As her mother describes it, "they took turns at her, doing—different things" (200). This revelation brings to light not only Sandy's trauma but that of her mother, who had known about her daughter's violation—she read about it in the girl's diary—but had said nothing to Sandy, and who has throughout the action refused to discuss the diary or its contents with Archer. The tension in the Sebastian household is sexually motivated, the marriage largely sexless, and its cause finally surfaces. About her knowledge of her daughter's rape, Bernice says, "It came as such a shock, I couldn't think clearly about it. I still can't" (200). Archer suddenly suspects the reason: "I wondered if the same sort of thing had ever happened to her" (200).

As the action moves toward its conclusion, it offers some small hope that the Sebastians might become a family. Bernice has faced the reality of their life: "Keith and I were exploiting each other and Sandy, and that's the opposite of loving each other" (198). Her husband has rejected what amounts to a ten-thousand-dollar bribe from Mrs. Hackett, in that act freeing himself of a largely self-imposed professional and economic bondage; as Archer observes, "The moral force required to part with the money generated more of the same in Sebastian" (214). His daughter, while still distrustful, looks "at her father with changing eyes" (214). Still, given the nature of the society of which they are a part, the future of the family is problematic. That society has been exposed as corrupt and corrupting, composed of victimizers and victims. Thus Archer's symbolic gesture in the final paragraph of the novel, as he destroys a $100,000 check meant to ensure his silence: "I tore it into small pieces and tossed the yellow confetti out the window. It drifted down on the short hairs and the long hairs, the potheads and the acid heads, draft dodgers and dollar chasers, swingers and walking wounded, idiot saints, hard cases, foolish virgins" (227).

The Instant Enemy contains as much "felt life" as any of the Archer novels; characters, scenes, and situations continue to haunt the reader long after he has finished the book. This despite the fact that the structure of the novel is seriously flawed. Archer's emotional focus throughout the action is on the fate of Davy Spanner and Sandy Sebastian. Once Davy is dead and Sandy placed in a position of possible reintegration with her parents, there remains only the tying together of the loose ends. Essentially this involves characters whom we either have no real interest in or actually find despicable. And while the remaining revelations explain more of Davy Spanner's life, they do not intensify the tragedy of his death. Indeed, by the time Archer gets to the Esau and Jacob story that is the source of most of the evil, neither he nor the reader really cares who did what and why. Everything is neatly worked out, but by this point Archer is just going through the motions. As serious as this structural flaw is, however, it does not mitigate the power of the real story.

The Goodbye Look

The Goodbye Look (1969), on the other hand, is a work nearly flawless in both conception and execution. In Macdonald's oeuvre it is, as T. R. Steiner has observed, "the tightest, cleanest, sparest of all."[7] As Steiner also points out, "more impressive than the book's image of life are the fact of its patternings and interlacements and its artistic finality."[8] *The Instant Enemy,* for all its structural problems, presents a vision of life as a raw and savage conflict, of human existence in midcentury America as a problem-riddled battle against mostly unseen enemies and often untraceable evil. The next Archer novel blunts the emotional force of that vision by presenting it through a multifaceted work rather than through an intensely focused narration. Technically superior to anything Macdonald had yet written, *The Goodbye Look* is, like *Black Money,* a beautifully crafted book that subordinates emotion to art, vision to pattern.

The novel opens swiftly, if quietly, as Archer is contacted by attorney John Truttwell on behalf of his neighbors and clients, Lawrence and Irene Chalmers. Chalmers, as Truttwell describes him, is a wealthy war hero and "in our instant society . . . the closest thing we have to an aristocrat," and his wife is "a hell of a good-looking woman" (5). From Mrs. Chalmers Archer learns that their concern is the theft of a gold Florentine box containing the letters her husband wrote to his mother during the war. He also perceives that the obvious suspect is the Chalmerses' son, Nick, a college student with a history of emotional problems, whom Mrs. Chalmers is intent on protecting from the scrutiny of the authorities.

Twelve pages after he begins his search for the gold box, Archer finds it in a motel room. The box, on the painted lid of which "a man and woman in skimpy antique clothes disported themselves" (28), he doesn't bother with, for he has begun to "sense that the theft of the box was just a physical accident of the case. Any magic it possessed, black or white or gold, was soaked up from the people who handled it" (28).

The rest of the novel follows Archer as he traces the elaborate pattern of relationships among the characters connected with the box. As he proceeds, he does less "detecting" than simply listening to the characters and to their stories, each of which has to some extent the "swooping certainty of a mind tracking on fantasy" (81). Admixtures of illusion, delusion, and confusion, of reality buried in time and covered with carefully tended fantasies, these stories accrue in Archer's memory, some settling firmly in place to extend the pattern begun by others, some altering that pattern to expose the violent incompatibility of many of its elements. These accounts of events and relationships continually reshape themselves, and the pattern they create continually shifts as its informing principles change, until finally the stories of six different families become one story.

As they must. For the tone and texture of the novel posit the inevitable interconnectedness of everything that Archer discovers. The burglary of the Chalmerses' home must be somehow connected with the burglary of the same house twenty years before, which resulted in the hit-and-run killing of Truttwell's wife by the fleeing burglars. Everything connects because everything arises from the same source, the same past, a past to which the characters can never return but from which they can never escape. This Archer confirms for himself early in the action. After examining the seedy hotel room of a car repossessor who fancies himself a private investigator, Archer walks on the beach, letting the ocean wind work on the depression caused by his "brief dip into Sidney Harrow's life . . . perhaps it reminded me too strongly of my own life" (34). For a moment the bracing breeze off the sea dispels his sense of his own fate and the failure of his own dreams: "The waves were collapsing like walls there, and I felt like a man escaping from his life" (34). But only for a moment. "You can't, of course," he observes, as he sees Harrow's car in a sand drift at the edge of the parking lot. Almost without looking, he knows what's inside it.

The "instant society" in *The Goodbye Look* is the creation of deceit and desire, dream and illusion, and held together by a complex structure of secrets. None of the characters is precisely what he presents himself to be; some are not who they pretend to be. Little is as it seems, yet all, finally, is as it must be. Finally the past and its truth will not stay hidden. Forces long restrained begin to erupt. Archer finds a body. Then he finds another. Old deaths take on new meaning, old relationships new significance. The characters continue to speak, Archer continues to listen, and the truth emerges.

The novel is pervaded by suffering and concerned with murders present and past, but it contains little overt violence. Here is Archer finding the first body: "I looked in through the rear window and saw the dead man huddled on the back seat with dark blood masking his face" (35); and here he finds the second: "There was a smell of burning from the kitchen. I found that a glass coffeemaker on an electric plate had boiled dry and cracked. Jean Trask was lying near it on the green vinyl floor" (105). And the only death that occurs "on stage": "The patrol cars stopped abruptly, ejecting four policemen who began to fire their revolvers at Shepherd. He went down flat on his face and slid a little. Then splashes on the back of his neck and down the back of his light coat were darker and realer than his slipping red wig" (189). The most savage incident in the book is a slap in the face, of which Archer calmly observes: "It wasn't the sort of thing that Truttwell should be doing" (242).

This deliberate muting of effects establishes the emotional tone and cadences for Archer's slow discovery of the truth of the central event in an action spread over more than twenty years. Fifteen years earlier an eight-year-old boy was abducted and sexually assaulted by a transient, whom the child killed. Except the boy wasn't really abducted. The "assault" was—probably, as this can never be made completely clear—merely a drunken gesture of paternal affection, for the man the boy killed was his own father. For reasons that are superficially "right" and justifiable by current psychological theory but that are actually the product of greed, guilt, and the need to protect an illusion, the boy's nominal father, his mother, and the psychiatrist who treats the boy hide the truth from him. That boy, Nick Chalmers, is condemned to fifteen years of emotional turmoil, until he at last sets out to learn the truth and precipitates four more deaths.

And what sort of human monster is responsible for all this, as well as for setting up Nick as the primary suspect in two murders? He is a man living a pathetic fantasy, a sick man who "without supportive therapy, and drugs" supplied by his psychiatrist would "probably have to be hospitalized" (234). A man who had a mental breakdown when he entered the military and who spent the war a few miles from home, writing to his mother "manly" letters in which he adopted a stoic and heroic persona, letters that he later read to an eight-year-old in an attempt to inculcate in the boy the "manly" virtues. Letters that he kept in a gold Florentine box.

That box, of course, is meant to suggest Pandora's—Macdonald even explicates the symbolism for the inattentive reader. But equally if more subtly symbolic are the two lovers who "disported themselves" on its lid, for the troubles and suffering set loose both arise from and are intensified by the way the characters love one another. Originally the gift of a husband to his wife, the box became the token of a liaison between lovers. For the daughter of the original owner, the box "stands for everything that has happened to my family. Our whole life went to pieces. Other people ended up with our money and our furniture and even our little objects of art" (136). What happens to that family is the result of the amours of a man appropriately named Eldon Swain. The misery of his wife and his lover, his son and his daughter, is the legacy of his "disporting." Throughout the novel, the golden box continues to gather meanings, until all come together in the flickering images of the past,

in an old home movie in which a poolside scene of parents and children frol-
icking in the water concludes with an image that projects the future of all of
them: "As if controlled by a documentary interest, the camera followed the
pair as Rita stood spraddled on the diving board, and Eldon Swain inserted
his head between her legs and lifted her. Tottering slightly, he carried her out
to the end of the board and stood for a long moment with his head projecting
from between her thighs like the head of a giant smiling baby being born"
(213–14).

In this image Macdonald fuses the psychosexual themes that the novel develops at every turn. Each of the characters is bound in an erotic relationship
with Freudian and generational implications, each is tied to images of the
past that shackle present action. Even Lew Archer is drawn into the web. His
affair with Moira Smitheram, attenuated as it is, nevertheless follows the pattern of all the romantic attachments in the novel. In their first personal conversation, for example, their sexual banter concludes with Archer's only half
facetious charge that Moira is arguing that he had "better marry again before
I get too old, or I won't have anybody to nurse me in my old age" (128). Two
pages later, at the edge of the ocean, Moira speaks: "'Come and get me,' she
said to it or me or someone else" (130); as the action makes clear, she is addressing all three. Then Archer describes a small event that suggests the nature and the fate of the relationship: "She was walking backward, trying to fit
her feet again into the prints she had made and not succeeding" (131). Although they later spend the night together, merging "our loneliness once
more, in something less than love but sweeter than self" (154), neither Moira
nor Archer can bring to the affair enough of themselves to give it consequence. Neither can escape the meaning of the footprints that have brought
each to the other. At the same time, neither can transform the present into
images created in the past. They can only go on, alone.

So will all the characters. Lives have been taken, lives have been destroyed. There is no happy ending, no settling of the unsettling, no
reunification of families. There is, finally, only truth, and understanding of
the truth. It is little consolation but, given the world Macdonald creates, it
is consolation enough.

For all the ambiguity that Macdonald shows lurking in the lives and relationships of these characters, and for all the complexity of the action, the
novel is remarkably coherent. This results from the economy and precision of
the narrative, from Macdonald's careful rendering of his material, from his
art. Steiner has analyzed this art in some detail: "Macdonald interlaces the
lives of at least six principal family groups. Although this is one of his most
complex plots . . . the lines remain remarkably clear. . . . As the reader keeps

constructing and having to reconstruct the relationships of characters—the identities, parallels, triangles—as the true configuration is slowly revealed, there is a dance of the whole that makes literary and moral sense."[9]

This "dance of the whole" is perhaps the most beautifully choreographed and aesthetically satisfying in Macdonald's oeuvre, its rhythms carefully controlled by suspense, revelation, and reversal, its cadences solemn and stately, its movement quietly tragic. Eschewing the easy effects available to the genre, Macdonald instead molds image and action, character and idea, into a structure that is the novel's meaning.

The Goodbye Look brought Macdonald the readership he had long worked for. Readers coming to his fiction for the first time found a thematic integrity and artistic sophistication that produced formal elegance and narrative eloquence, an intricate pattern of literal and symbolic meaning. Those familiar with his work found one more instance in which he had, through the exercise of his art, transformed the American detective novel into a medium for the expression of a vision not about crime but about life.

Chapter Eight
Underground Art

The success of *The Goodbye Look* brought Macdonald both personal gratification and the professional challenge of following a popular and critical success. Writing to his editor about his next novel, Macdonald explained his problem, described his solution, and assessed the results: "There is always moral pain involved in following a great success, and I never worked so hard on a book in my life. The main thing is that it's different from the others . . . and not a self-imitation. Looking it over in some coolness, I think it may get me some new readers. The nature of the action, fire and flight, brings the energy up to the surface and should make it more readily available to the ordinary reader."[1] Underlying these remarks is Macdonald's long-held conviction that a work of fiction could be at once popular and serious, that a detective novel could aim at a wide audience of ordinary readers and at the same time appeal to those of more sophisticated literary tastes. The novel of which he spoke, *The Underground Man* (1971), validated this conviction, equaling the previous novel in sales and at the same time receiving even more serious critical appreciation.

Arguably Macdonald's "greatest achievement," *The Underground Man* is clearly the best example of his mature "underground" art—a detective novel that works as a straightforward account of Lew Archer's successful pursuit of a solution to the "labyrinthian riddles of human violence," while at the same time it presents an aesthetically controlled and highly patterned meditation on the "mysteries of human guilt and hate and love."[2]

At first glance, *The Underground Man* seems much like several of Macdonald's other novels. The immediate concern of both Archer and the reader is the fate of a young boy, the mystery involves the fate of a character who never appears in the action, and the action is informed by a thematic deliberation on the problems of familial relations. Nevertheless, *The Underground Man* is indeed "different from the others"—from the other Archer novels in the precision and intricacy of its art, from other detective novels in the presence of that art, and from all American fiction in the exercise of this art in a detective novel.

Fire and Flight

The Underground Man opens with an economical chapter that introduces the volatile mix of character, issue, and circumstance soon to explode into the case. Awakened in the predawn of West Los Angeles by a "hot wind," Archer is then reawakened by "scrub jays . . . dive-bombing my window sill."[3] He goes out to feed the birds peanuts and is soon joined by a small boy. Man and boy feed the birds and talk, Archer responding to Ronny Broadhurst's uneasy questions about the jays' violence with reassurances that they are fighting over the food, that they do not kill each other, and that they sometimes kill the young of other species but that they don't kill children. As Archer tosses peanuts for the boy to catch in his mouth, they are suddenly interrupted by a "grown up version of the boy" (5), who comes from the street, smoking a cigarillo; at the same moment, a woman whom Archer describes as "pretty enough to make me conscious that I hadn't shaved" (5) steps out of a nearby apartment.

Stanley and Jean Broadhurst immediately fall to verbal battle, as "raucously, bloodlessly" (4) as the jays, with sexual weapons. Broadhurst accuses his wife of having left him for a tryst with Archer, while she demands to know if "the girl" is still at their home. At one point Broadhurst, on the edge of irrational violence, moves to strike his son. Archer pulls the boy away from the threatened blow, ignores Broadhurst's insults and his own impulse to violence, and attempts to mediate the dispute. Stanley Broadhurst and his son finally leave to visit the boy's grandmother in Santa Teresa. Archer and Jean then try to talk about the situation, but "the scene he had made still echoed dismally in the air" (8). Then Stanley returns for Ronny's toys; at the second parting of the Broadhursts, Archer notes that, "they sounded like a couple who never expected to see each other again. . . . I wanted to stop Broadhurst and bring the boy back. But I didn't" (9). Instead, he climbs the stairs of the building and moves around to its front, where he sees Ronny in the front seat of a Ford convertible with a "blond girl or woman" (9); a few minutes later he begins to descend the stairs: "Halfway down I paused and leaned on the handrail and told myself that I was descending into trouble: a pretty young woman with a likable boy and a wandering husband. A hot wind was blowing in my face" (9).

In these six pages Macdonald prepares for the events to follow. Stanley Broadhurst's violent instability, his wife's anger and pain, their son's confused vulnerability, the unexplained presence of the "blond girl or woman"— all combine with Archer's attraction toward Jean Broadhurst and his sympathetic affection for the little boy to create his foreboding, his prescience of impending disaster. Less than forty pages later that disaster has struck: Stanley Broadhurst lies murdered in a shallow grave near the family cabin in the hills above his mother's home, a grave he apparently dug himself; a fire started by his cigarillo rages over the hills and canyons around Santa Teresa; and both the blond girl and Ronny Broadhurst are missing. Archer has a client, a case, and a riddle of violence.

The surface action of which Macdonald spoke proceeds swiftly. As the fire threatens the Broadhurst home, Archer begins his inquiry. Its object is not the murderer of Stanley Broadhurst, however. The detective's primary motivation is his concern for Ronny Broadhurst. From Fritz Snow, the emotionally feeble gardener, he learns that the blond girl has fled with Ronny in Fritz's old car. Dodging—and at one point helping to fight—the fire, Archer follows his leads, which consist of an old copy of *Green Mansions* and a borrowed Mercedes. Soon he identifies the girl as Sue Crandall, the seventeen-year-old daughter of an affluent Los Angeles couple, Martha and Lester Crandall. Almost as quickly he links her to Jerry Kilpatrick, the disaffected son of Santa Teresa real estate developer Brian Kilpatrick.

Sue Crandall, Archer has learned from Jean Broadhurst, has "strange" (24) eyes and has told Ronny a bizarre fantasy in which a little girl's "parents were killed by monsters and the little girl was carried off by a big bird like a condor. She said that had happened to her when she was his age" (25). Jean ultimately concludes that "she was afraid" (25). Tracing the Mercedes, Archer learns that the previous night Sue climbed the mast of the boat on which Jerry Kilpatrick was staying and threatened to kill herself.

With little difficulty Archer locates Jerry at the Santa Teresa marina, where he has been living on the sloop *Ariadne*. Jerry, "a very hostile young man" (75) with eyes "like damaged glass" (76), refuses Archer entry into the marina. But nearby the detective finds the car in which Sue Crandall had fled. After dark he sneaks aboard the boat and discovers Sue and Ronny hiding in one of the bunks. Not a word is spoken. Sue "looked at me from some other place, almost as if she was ready to die or perhaps already had" (79). The little boy she is silencing "lay still beside her. Even his round blue eyes were perfectly still" (80). Then Jerry Kilpatrick appears behind Archer with a gun and knocks him out. The detective regains consciousness on the slip. The sloop is gone.

This encounter with the two teenagers establishes the emotional background for much of Archer's later action, for it makes clear that in some important sense both Sue and Jerry are victims. Because of her bizarre behavior, Archer suspects that Sue may be on drugs and that she may not have taken them willingly. And despite the fact that Jerry has attacked him, Archer knows that he himself invited the attack. Coupled with the fact that this is not a standard kidnapping, and indeed may not be a kidnapping at all, these considerations prevent him from thinking too harshly of Sue and Jerry. The wisdom of this attitude is quickly borne out as, shifting the focus of his investigation, Archer talks to the parents of the missing teenagers. In these discussions he learns little that helps his search but a great deal that explains the general thrust of their actions.

The parents are concerned for their children but unforthcoming about the real problems plaguing the families; at the same time they are quick to blame everyone but themselves. As Brian Kilpatrick puts it, "We're losing a whole generation. They're punishing us for bringing them into the world" (84). But Archer sees in Kilpatrick an alcoholic who rages against his son's use of drugs, a man with "a salesman's insight into human weakness" (86) but none into his own. As Kilpatrick douses himself in booze and placates his drunken, bikini-clad "fiancé," the detective catches "a glimpse of the broken seriousness which lived in him like a spoiled priest in hiding" (89).

What he finds in the Crandall's Los Angeles home is equally revealing. Martha Crandall is a carefully constructed personality whose veneer of affluent artifice cannot hide her earthy sensuality and rough origins. As Mrs. Crandall describes Sue's "really good life" with "every advantage" (101), Archer perceives that "she was one of those dreaming blonds who couldn't bear to face a change in her life. One of those waiting mothers who would sit forever beside the phone but didn't know what to say when it finally rang" (102). Talking with Sue's father, Archer finds in the man's hands the key to his life and his current pain: "He had spent his life, I thought, working his way to the top of a small hill which his daughter had abandoned in one jump" (102–3). And the detective has an insight into the situation: "It was often the same problem—an unreality so bland and smothering that the children tore loose and impaled themselves on the spikes of any reality that offered. Or made their own unreality with drugs" (104).

Thematically reinforcing the point, the next chapter has Archer following another clue to the seedy Star Motel and the young-old junkie who whimsically calls herself Elegant, who confirms that Sue Crandall had been fed LSD. From the "dilapidated girl" with "bruises on her arms and thighs like the hash-marks of hard service" (119) he learns enough to point the case in two quite different directions: back toward Santa Teresa and Fritz Snow's mother, and to the San Francisco Bay Peninsula and a "big old house in the woods" (118). Near his apartment, Archer returns and goes to bed. The next day he awakes to feed the jays, which swoop into the yard like "a flashing blue explosion-in-reverse that put the morning world together again. But the central piece was missing" (121). He sets off again in search of Ronny Broadhurst.

By evening he has found all three of the youngsters, but not through his tracking skill. After setting another detective in search of the house on the peninsula, Archer spends most of the day in and around Santa Teresa; as crews battle the fire (Archer's descriptions are larded with martial images and metaphors), he talks again with the adults involved in the case—Jean Broadhurst, Mrs. Snow, Brian Kilpatrick, the Crandalls. More information comes to the surface, facades of personality shift, hidden relationships suggest themselves. Archer begins to see that the killing of Stan Broadhurst and the flight of the young people is inextricably linked with long-buried patterns of crime and love which just as inextricably link the various families. What he gains is not evidence but understanding, so that when he finds Sue, Jerry, and Ronny he can deal with them on the basis of the truth that he has discovered: they are "a generation whose elders had been poisoned, like the pelicans, with a kind of moral DDT that damaged the lives of their young" (226).

The case breaks. The *Ariadne* has run aground and is being destroyed in the surf near the peninsula. The three young people have fled to a motel owned by Susan's father and from there headed for the Sausalito home of Jerry's long-vanished mother, Ellen Strome Kilpatrick, who was thought to have run off fifteen years before with Stanley Broadhurst's father, Leo. Archer gets to the house first and talks with Ellen Storm, as she calls herself. He finds her a romantic and slightly dotty artist who paints, she says, "things that don't reflect the light—spiritual conditions"; to Archer her paintings resemble "serious contusions and open wounds" (200).

The young people arrive, but a terror-stricken Sue drives off with Ronny. Archer follows. The girl is stopped at the Golden Gate Bridge. Archer sees her running across it with the little boy. He pursues. "Susie looked back once. She let go of Ronny's hand, moved to the railing, and went over. I thought for a sickening instant that she had taken the final plunge. Then I saw her light hair blowing above the railing" (208). Largely because of Ronny's trust in him, Archer is able to talk Sue back, but not before the girl "inclined her head to one side and looked down over her shoulder, into the depth of my lying and the terrible depth of her rage" (210).

The flight is over. Reconciliations, of a sort, follow. As Sue and Martha Crandall meet, Archer feels "a flicker" of hope. Sue, who in addition to witnessing at least one murder has been drugged and raped, will get professional help. Her mother will get it too, and will tell her daughter the truth about both their lives. Jerry will stay with his mother, which Archer realizes is not a "solution. She was far gone in solitude, and he was too old to need a mother, really. He had to live out his time of trouble, as she had" (226). No charges will be brought against the alienated adolescents: "They seem to have thought they were rescuing Ronny from the adult world. To a certain extent it was true" (234). Archer returns the boy to his mother, then drives both back to Los Angeles. He has another flicker of hope: "I hoped that Ronny's life wouldn't turn back toward his father's death as his father's life had turned, in a narrowing circle. I wished the boy a benign failure of memory" (273).

The Underground Man

Near the end of the novel, Archer acknowledges that "when I returned the boy Ronny to his mother, I had really accomplished what I set out to do" (252). But three homicides remain unsolved, and Archer cannot walk away; "there was a winding symmetry in the case" (253) that, like the stairs he descends to the morgue, compels him to follow. But this symmetry is as much imposed on the case by Archer's will to understand as it arises from the events. By the end of the novel, he has presented a version of the events and their motivation, but it is only a version. In Archer's version of things Macdonald accounts, more or less, for the killings and all that surround them, and so fulfills the requirements of the genre. While plausible, however, Archer's version of "reality" actually explains little. The real questions raised in the novel remain unanswered, the real mystery remains unsolved.

Early in the novel Archer learns that Stanley Broadhurst has long been obsessed with the disappearance of his father, whom he believes to have run off with an unidentified woman fifteen years before. At the end of the novel, Archer has found Broadhurst's remains and explained his disappearance; he has not, however, really explained the man himself. Everyone has something to say about Leo Broadhurst, and it is clear that some time after his marriage he began actively womanizing. Why this happened is not so clear. Some people blame his wife, while others accuse him. The truth seems to lie somewhere between his killer's hysterical claim that "he was a wicked man, a cheat and a fornicator" (272) and the testimony of an old lover: "He couldn't stand to be alone. He had to have someone with him in order to feel really alive" (202). The precise nature of that truth, the real reason he did what he did, remains a mystery.

Examining Stanley's office, Archer observes the "gray steel filing cabinet standing like a cenotaph" (21) in which the younger man had kept the records of his search for his father. Jean Broadhurst has already given her explanation of her husband's obsession: "He seems to feel that when his father ran out on him, it robbed his life of its meaning. . . . He's angry at his father for abandoning him; at the same time he misses him and loves him. The two together can be paralyzing" (18). Later Archer reads a letter to Stanley from his minister, filled with excellent advice about the need to allow the past to remain past and to concentrate on life in the present. Yet the minister cannot explain why people do what they do. He can offer only a Pascalian enigma: "The heart has its reasons that the reason does not know" (96). For all the various "reasons" provided by the characters in novel, the novel itself comes to the same Pascalian conclusion.

As the Santa Teresa fire advances and retreats under the direction of its own energy and the caprice of the wind, so Archer moves between past and present under the impetus of the information he uncovers. Pursuing Jerry, Sue, and Ronny across the Southern California landscape of the present, he discovers in the grudging admissions and painful confessions of their parents several old and intimate connections among the families. Most of these connections are motivated, but their deeper reasons remain ambiguous. It is clear, however, that although the immediate case began when Stanley Broadhurst placed an ad in the *San Francisco Chronicle* seeking information about his missing father, the real case began long before, with the sexual adventures of Leo Broadhurst and the muddle of love that trapped the participants as well as innocent bystanders like his son.

The "underground" plot of the novel, as in many of the Archer novels, is, as William Goldman put it, a bit extremely, "so ramified, Delphic and dark" that its "telling . . . is impossible."[4] The complexity of *The Underground Man* is suggested by Bruce Cook's assessment of Macdonald's handling of the murder of Leo Broadhurst: "He asks us to believe that when Stan Broadhurst's father was murdered up on the hilltop behind his home, there were eight people around (and a piece of earth-moving equipment, no less, brought in to dispose of the body). These eight, all of whom knew something about the murder, had conflicting interests in the matter but nevertheless kept silence for fifteen years until Lew Archer came along and got them talking."[5] The tone of Cook's remarks conveys his incredulity. The fact is, however, that this is not what Macdonald would have us believe, necessarily, but what Archer would have himself believe.

The denouement of the novel is Archer's careful and elaborate construction, consisting of as much speculation and surmise as verifiable fact and forthright admission. Archer has incontestable evidence about the method of the murders—Leo Broadhurst was shot with a .22, but the actual cause of death was stabbing. The rest, however, is based on the memories of characters who throughout the action confuse one murder with another, on the assertions of others whom the novel has shown to be inveterate or pathological liars, or on the accusations of Archer that are not satisfactorily answered. Of the identity of the killer there is no doubt; it is established by a confession. But the real reasons many of the characters act as they do, as well as many of the details of the action, remain mysterious.

One of those apparently "around" the murder of Leo Broadhurst was his young son, Stanley. The night Broadhurst "disappeared," he and his wife, Elizabeth, had a violent argument about Leo's womanizing, an argument apparently precipitated by Elizabeth Broadhurst's fear that her husband was leaving her. Both Stanley and the housekeeper, Mrs. Snow, overheard much of the confrontation, which ended with Leo roaring off in his sports car toward the mountain cabin where a woman awaited him. Mrs. Broadhurst put her son to bed and followed her husband on foot, with one of her father's old pistols. Stanley followed his mother and heard a shot that she later explained she had fired at an owl. All this information, however, comes from Mrs. Snow, who throughout the novel skillfully twists facts to her advantage. Elizabeth Broadhurst later confirms the outline of the events, but the detail, the reality, remains obscure. What is certain is that the boy never saw or heard from his father again. Thus his adult obsession was not simply with finding his father but, again according to Mrs. Snow, "trying to prove that his daddy was alive" (242) and that his father had not been killed by his mother.

Another of those "around" the night of Leo Broadhurst's murder was Susan Crandall, then three years old. Susan was in the loft of the cabin while her mother was below making love with Leo (one of the truths Mrs. Crandall will tell her daughter is that Leo Broadhurst was probably Sue's natural father). Sue's memories of that night surface in the strange drug-structured bedtime story she tells Ronny, and again when Archer questions her about the murder of Stanley Broadhurst. Her acid- and anxiety-laced ramblings mix the accounts of the two murders, as well as of her rape, in a "regressive fairy tale voice" (214), but Archer gets enough out of it to be able to ask Martha Crandall the right questions.

Mrs. Crandall, with whom Broadhurst was going to run off, knows that he was shot; she does not know that he is dead. Elizabeth Broadhurst knows that her husband was shot, because she shot him; she does not know that he was also stabbed. Fritz Snow knows that Broadhurst is dead, because he helped bury him; but he thinks that Broadhurst was killed by Martha (Marty Nickerson) Crandall, whom he pathetically adores. Albert Sweetner, who lived with the Snows, also participated in the burial; his knowledge of the events costs him his life fifteen years later. All of these characters know something of what happened; none of them knows it all. Only when Stanley puts his ad in the newspaper do they start talking, not to Archer but to each other. Only after Stanley is killed does Archer begin asking questions. And even then it is less Archer's interrogations than the events in the present that force versions of the truth about the past to the surface.

Archer finds Leo Broadhurst, the underground man, in the same grave his son occupied, but deeper in the earth; in the buried sports car with an "odor of corruption," Leo Broadhurst is "all bones and teeth" (239). But there is another underground man, a man who apparently engineered the last bitter confrontation between Leo and Elizabeth Broadhurst in a misguided attempt to get his own wife to return to him, and the only one to profit by the murder. For fifteen years, Brian Kilpatrick has used his knowledge to bleed Elizabeth Broadhurst of her money. His wife, however, did not return, and his extortion cost him his son. Through most of the novel, Kilpatrick is a figure of some sympathy. In his final confrontation with Archer, he denies the detective's accusations, insisting that he was "an innocent bystander" (260). The novel makes clear that, in one sense at least, this is true; it also makes clear that the real nature of Kilpatrick's involvement in the events is obscure. But Archer's final view of Kilpatrick reveals the man's condition: "He was running short of desire and hope. The aura of success had deserted him, and he was looking more and more like a loser" (260). Brian Kilpatrick returns to his home and kills himself.

But Kilpatrick did not kill the others. Mrs. Snow killed Leo Broadhurst in revenge for the injury she believed he did to her son: "Frederick has never been the same since" (272). Perhaps. Certainly Frederick "Fritz" Snow, with his confused sympathies and harelip, his secret sexual desires and constant fear, has "emotional problems. Also genetic ones" (263). But Fritz himself offers a different explanation for his condition. "I keep remembering when Digger got my daddy . . . when they buried him out at the cemetery. I could hear the dirt plunking down on the coffin" (241). Thus his mother's motive is suspect, and at best partial. Ultimately she cannot provide a convincing and conclusive reason for murdering Leo Broadhurst. She killed Stanley Broadhurst and Albert Sweetner to cover up the first murder, Archer assumes, but he does not really ask about her reasons. And he neatly—perhaps a bit too neatly—sums her up: "She was one of those paranoid souls who kept her conscience clear by blaming everything on other people. Her violence and malice appeared to her as emanations from the external world" (272). Like many of his explanations, however, this doesn't explain very much. In fact, what explanations the novel contains come not from the detective or the other characters but from the movement and structure of the work.

Art and Meaning

The opening chapter of the *The Underground Man* not only sets the stage for the action to follow but also establishes the principles and patterns according to which the novel will be structured. Through a careful orchestration of incident and image, this chapter functions as an overture announcing the themes that will inform all the events to follow. The rest of the narrative will present variations on these themes, altering and adjusting Archer's perceptions of the characters and modifying the meaning of their acts without, however, achieving the resolution that "wraps up" the classic, rationalistic detective story that regards plot as an end in itself. Thus while Lew Archer "solves" the case, the human and moral consequences of the novel's conclusion remain profoundly problematic.

The scene that Stanley Broadhurst creates at the beginning of *The Underground Man* involves a highly charged emotional triangle that pivots around the innocent character at its center, young Ronny Broadhurst. Stanley's ire is raised by his suspicion of a relationship between Archer, Ronny, and Jean—a relationship at once imaginary and incipient. Jean fears the violence imminent in the struggle of Archer and Stanley over Ronny, and is angry at the presence in her husband's life of the "blond girl or woman." (Ronny is last seen sitting between Stanley and this woman.) Archer attempts to mediate the dispute between wife and husband primarily because of its obvious effect on the boy.

To point out that the implicit sexual and parental themes make this first chapter a sort of dour dance to the tune of a Freudian family romance is to observe the obvious. To suggest, however, that by finding the central theme of the novel in Freudian psychocosmology we have done anything but bring to the forefront Macdonald's ultimate subject is to confuse the medium with the message. The theoretical construct we call the Freudian family romance does not provide a solution to the problems that the novel raises, but simply a frame for the presentation and a vocabulary for the expression of these problems. For Macdonald, Freud "rendered our moral vision forever ambivalent," and it is precisely in the expression of this ambivalence that his art is rooted.

A sexual/parental triangle surfaces on nearly every page of the novel, informing in one sense or another the relations between all the characters. Sometimes it is explicit, as in the obvious tension between Jean Broadhurst and her mother-in-law and their differences over Stanley. More often a number of triangles are implied, as in Elizabeth Broadhurst's complex relationships with her dead father, her dead husband, her son, and her grandson; emotionally she stands paralyzed at the central point where the apexes of these triangles meet. While each of these triangles represents a relationship charged by the energies of the same Freudian concept, each is different, and none in any significant way explains the others. For example, Mrs. Broadhurst has lived her life in sexual and emotional thrall to her father, of whom she writes "Robert Driscoll Falconer, Jr., was a god come down to earth in human guise." About that writing Archer notes "toward the end, the handwriting went to pieces. It straggled across the lined yellow page like a defeated army" (147). In one way or another, most of the characters in the novel are in the same predicament, suffering the actual or symbolic loss of a parent. The novel presents no fewer than four boys who have been abandoned by their fathers. Leo Broadhurst "abandons" young Stanley; Stanley disappears, leaving his own son. Both Leo and Stanley have in fact vanished into the grave—the same grave, it turns out. Jerry Kilpatrick's father, on the other hand, is very much alive, but in his ultimate if concealed corruption he has abandoned Jerry to the life of the beach bum. And the death of Fritz's father has left him at the mercy of an overprotective and excessively religious mother.

The meaning of all this, and of the novel as a whole, is at best uncertain. It resides not in what Archer tells us but in what the action that he narrates shows us. The many triangular relationships come together to form a thematic collage in which Macdonald would have us observe the complex and confusing nature of the parent-child bond. The novel would have us see what it means to be a parent and a child, to see that the problems of such a relationship are at once inherent and insoluble, that they have their roots in the ever-disappearing and unrecoverable past. While Archer can find "flickers" of hope in all this, the novel suggests that he finds something hopeful only because he must. Macdonald has deliberately shaped the novel to make clear that we are to trust the tale rather than the teller. This is not, however, irony at Archer's expense. Lew Archer is the teller of this tale, but he is also a character in it, one with deeply personal attachments to the other characters— especially to Jean and Ronny Broadhurst; thus he will attempt to project their future in terms that he can live with, he will solve the case so that it cannot plague Ronny Broadhurst, he will wish the boy a "benign failure of memory." The structure of the novel, however, gives us a more detached and less optimistic view.

Nowhere is this more clear than in the novel's conclusion. And no part of the novel has been more misread. Jerry Speir, for example, argues that "when careful, concerned research by Archer, the democratic hero, restores sanity and hope to his psychically injured fellow human beings, the skies open and the healing, renewing rains descend. It is in that rain and in Archer's friendship with the child, Ronny, that the author finds his most powerful symbols for the expression of an optimistic declaration on the future."[6] Others, like Geoffrey Hartman, focus on the final paragraph in the novel, "when we find Lew Archer lingering with Stanley Broadhurst's widow and her young son . . . for one moment the family exists and the detective is the father."[7] Hartman at least notes that the moment is ephemeral, but other readers seem not to have noticed. There is, finally, nothing especially hopeful, symbolically or otherwise, about the ending of *The Underground Man.*

The fire, of course, is the central symbol of the book; with it, as Hartman notes, Macdonald combines "ecological and moral contamination."[8] Through most of the action, the fire ravages the landscape and threatens the city, occasionally consuming homes "as if picked out at random" (143). But while the effort to contain and extinguish the flames is massive, even its success will not eliminate the danger to the city. As Brian Kilpatrick prophetically observes, "the worst is yet to come. . . . The first real rain and we'll all be drowning in mud" (130). At the novel's end the rain has come, putting out the fire but also dumping tons of mud on Kilpatrick's house; the Broadhurst house, which survived the fire but for a scorching, is in even greater peril, for the creek behind it "had become a turbulent dark river, large enough to float fallen trees. Several of them had formed a natural dam which was backing up the water behind the house" (261). The sequence of biblical disasters has been reversed; now the flood follows the fire.

As for Archer, Jean Broadhurst, and Ronny somehow reconstituting the family, here too Macdonald forces us to see the conclusion as troubled and only temporary. Through the novel Archer does become a father figure to the boy; indeed, the night before he returns Ronny to his mother, the detective sleeps "across the door of Ronny's room" (232). Nevertheless, Archer's relationship with Jean Broadhurst is characterized by two constant perceptions: that he is "half in love with her, partly because she was Ronny's mother but also because she was beautiful and young" (154); and that there is something essentially unreal about her. Continually he sees her as "an actress" (148).

Finally Jean and Archer have nothing real to offer each other. And all Archer can offer Ronny is a wish, the hope that the past will not force his life in upon itself. But like his other hopes, this too is but a flicker. For the story Archer narrates tells us that the lives of Ronny's parents and grandparents will in some powerful but not always explicable way make the boy's own life other than he might want it. They must, for in the world of *The Underground Man,* and indeed all Macdonald's later fiction, that is what it means to be human.

Chapter Nine
The Legacy

Ross Macdonald wrote twenty-four novels in thirty years. This is a trifling number, of course, compared to the output of writers of formulaic fiction like Erle Stanley Gardner and Max Brand. That most of Macdonald's works—and especially the eighteen narrated by Lew Archer—are generic rather than formulaic, novels rather than programmatic exercises in fiction, makes the number more impressive. I have argued that several of the Archer books are as good as anything in the American detective novel and stand as evidence of the possibilities for quality in the genre. Unfortunately, this is not the case with the last two novels.

The End

Commentators have had a great deal to say about Macdonald's two final Archer novels, finding in them more intricate elaborations of his central themes as well as noteworthy insights into American society and culture in the 1970s. These the books certainly contain, along with much that is first-rate in characterization and language. What few remark upon, however, is the simple but unavoidable fact that neither *Sleeping Beauty* nor *The Blue Hammer* is remotely as good as many of the previous novels. Fascinating as each may be in terms of the lives of both their author and their narrator, neither is a successful novel.

Sleeping Beauty (1973) has elicited a great deal of praise from Macdonald's academic critics. Jerry Speir, for example, calls it a "powerful book,"[1] and Peter Wolfe considers it "Macdonald's deepest and perhaps best novel."[2] This critical approbation results, I think, from the fact that the novel lends itself nicely to the theses that these critics emphasize in their discussions about Macdonald's work and career; certainly the novel has special pertinence to thematic considerations of Macdonald's fiction. Beyond that, the primary focus of these critics is not so much on the novel as an action as on the acts, insights, and sociosexual predicament of Lew Archer. *Sleeping Beauty*, however, is not a collection of essays or observations or insights; it is a novel, and as such it is seriously flawed.

One reviewer noted that "we have two books here: a professionally crafted and largely satisfying detective story, to which has been welded a tentative overlay of Larger Things—a literary pretension that somewhat vitiates a plausible fiction."[3] In fact, the problem with the novel is just the opposite. It is an implausible fiction, a detective novel so poorly crafted that it renders some of the accompanying thematic discourse cumbersome, obvious, and—because it is unattached to any represented action—pretentious. The same reviewer insisted that the novel "absorbs the willing reader in complication upon convolution, adroitly flooding in false leads right to the end. If you care to play it like a chess game, it's a good one."[4] This is precisely what it isn't.

Sleeping Beauty is rather a story that requires coincidences of massive proportions to begin and to continue, a noncase that becomes a murder case only through more coincidences, an investigation of herrings so red that the author doesn't bother to explain them. Macdonald himself insisted that the detective novel required a "hard, logical structure," but here the underlying logic is fuzzy and gapped, the underpinning as gooey as the oil that blackens the Pacific Point beaches. The emotional structure of the book is equally confused. At its center is Laural Lennox Russo, a twenty-five-year old woman whom Archer accidentally meets on an oily beach and by whom he is immediately smitten. When she disappears, Archer 'manufactures' a case and discovers crimes old and new, but he never does discover, either literally or figuratively, the object of his obsession. As Bruccoli notes, "the plot loses track of the missing girl; she returns of her own accord, and it is lamely explained that she has been 'wandering around.'"[5] As a detective novel, *Sleeping Beauty* is inept; because it is a detective novel, it cannot be successful as anything else.

The Blue Hammer (1976) is much the same. Macdonald's critics have much to say about the themes the novel presents, and even more about Lew Archer's possible resolution of his alienation through a romantic relationship with a young journalist, but they say little about the story itself, and for good reason. Bruccoli makes a valiant effort to justify the novel's obvious weakness, arguing that Macdonald's "serious readers" had been "trained" to anticipate his plots, so that the "literary experience" had become "a guessing game"; this, Bruccoli would have it, "was not the result of a diminution of Millar's art . . . but the inevitable concomitant of his exploration of ritualized themes, which had become archetypal myths."[6]

This is ingenious but unpersuasive. 'Trained' or not, the serious reader of *The Blue Hammer* immediately perceives the underlying nature of the apparent mystery, so that it is not a mystery at all. It is instead an obvious and not especially skillful manipulation of characters and events toward a not very important revelation. The 'literary experience' is not a 'guessing game' but a deepening confusion as to what Macdonald might have thought he was doing with a story whose mystery is at once transparent and filled with loose ends. This final novel is indeed a diminution of Ross Macdonald's art.

The Achievement

Precisely why Macdonald's last two novels are as they are we, of course, will never know. *Sleeping Beauty* shows subtle signs that its author had perhaps taken a bit too seriously some of the fulsome commentary his previous works had provoked, that in it Macdonald was more interested in the quality of Archer's observations than in the coherence of his "imagined action in imagined retrospect." *The Blue Hammer,* on the other hand, seems a work by an author past the peak of his power. In any case, that they are unsuccessful does not alter the nature and significance of Macdonald's achievement overall.

Ross Macdonald not only raised the American detective novel to a new level of artistic excellence, but in doing so he also saved the genre from degeneration into the sort of standard and often silly tales that still fill the paperback racks. And he did it not by writing something other than detective novels or by somehow "transcending" the American detective novel but by writing excellent detective novels. As Sheldon Sacks notes, Macdonald's "quality and worth depend precisely on the degree to which he has realized magnificently potentialities always latent in detective stories."[7]

About that quality and worth there should be no misunderstanding.

As part of his definition of the "Great Tradition," F. R. Leavis argued that the major writers are those who "change the possibilities of the art for practitioners and readers."[8] This Macdonald certainly did, as writers who followed his lead have been quick to acknowledge. As Robert B. Parker observes, "in his craft and his integrity he made the detective form a vehicle for high seriousness."[9] And Dennis Lynds has detailed Ross Macdonald's influence and importance. Macdonald, Lynds maintains, opened up the genre by bringing it out of the Chandlerian "mean streets" and into the noncriminal milieu; he brought to it a psychological and social realism that transformed it into a "world the reader had to recognize as part and parcel of his own," a world inhabited by "the people next door, the neighbor up the block. That was the step Ross Macdonald took and gave to the writers to come after. . . . Wherever the next step is, it will be possible only because Ross Macdonald went before. We would not, probably could not, write the way we do and will if he had not written."[10]

Clearly Macdonald changed the possibilities for the art for both writers and readers of the American detective novel. For writers he not only demonstrated, as Lynds testifies, that the genre was not limited to stories of professional crime, but he also proved that the form could be what he said in his "manifesto" he wanted it to be—literate and adult. This in itself changed the American detective novel for those who would practice it, for by writing literate and adult novels Macdonald eventually attracted a different audience— the literate and adult—for whom these new writers could write. For these new readers, on the other hand, he provided a fiction that produced a double effect, combining the pleasure that comes from the detective story and the satisfaction that comes from the novel.

He did this in two ways. First, he developed the human aspect of the "hard, logical structure" of the detective novel, transforming it from the presentation of a logical puzzle into "a vehicle of meaning," expanding plot from a narrated sequence of events into a mode of emotional and intellectual apprehension. As George Grella has astutely observed, "the books seem, at times, to consist entirely of plot, to be about their plots, to be in fact all plot."[11] And all meaning. So integrated are these plots that those of us who would summarize or encapsulate them for purposes of critical discussion must to some extent falsify them. In the best of Macdonald's novels, plot is action that defines character, and character is attitude that qualifies action, so that the work develops in patterns that alter and reinforce meaning.

The other way Macdonald changed the art of the detective novel was to bring to it the techniques developed in and normally reserved for other kinds of novels. I have tried in this study to point out how Macdonald's rhetorical practices, his careful manipulation of the reader's response, employs the traditional suspense of the detective novel to bring the reader to a deeper view of certain basic human situations. His success in this enterprise results to a considerable extent from his use of the specific point of view he created through the use of Lew Archer as narrator, as well as his effective employment of structural, spatial, and symbolic devices more commonly found in serious fiction.

There are two other aspects of his art that appeal to this more literate readership. The first and more obvious is Macdonald's use of language. Among his critics the efficacy and value of his style is a subject of some debate. While my own view of this matter is implicit in this study, I have not explicitly joined the discussion, preferring instead to quote liberally from the fiction and let the language speak for itself. Not even his most severe critics, however, would deny that Macdonald had a masterful control over the English sentence and that he could make it do some marvelous things.

The second is less obvious, a matter of what we might call the prevailing authorial attitude of the novels. We might also call it ideology. And we might identify it as academic liberalism. The fact is that the Archer novels frame and discuss many of their themes in precisely those terms in which the educated liberal is accustomed to seeing them framed—Freudian psychology, racial amelioration, ecological conservatism, for example. Many of the ideological underpinnings of Macdonald's fiction are in full view in his early, non-Archer works; in the later books the same structure of thought and attitude, while sometimes less easily identified, supports the action and dictates much of Archer's commentary and evaluation.

The American detective novel, of course, had been in its popular form conservative, even reactionary, sometimes even fascist. Ross Macdonald, even more than Chandler, made it accessible to more liberal attitudes. Thus L. L. Lee can say of Macdonald's fiction—wrongly, I think—that "on one level, he is suggesting that money makes us act immorally, but on another more significant one he is asserting that morally the individual does not matter to the collectivity. In sum, Macdonald as artist is a critic of the individual as well as of the society."[12]

In identifying the ideological basis of Macdonald's fiction, I do not mean to disparage it. On the other hand, I do not believe that it has much to do with the quality of Ross Macdonald's art. All narrative art must contain ideas; both the ideas professed by the characters and the ideas embodied in patterns of action constitute what Aristotle called the element of thought in imitative fictions. But if we read fiction for ideas we are bound both to be disappointed and to misread it. The ideas in Macdonald's fiction are neither new nor profound. Indeed, few if any novels have anything significantly new or profound to say about their subjects. Novels—at least mimetic, "realistic" novels—are not coded or embellished discourse whose purpose is the transmission of ideas. They are imitations of human actions designed to make us respond in specific ways so that we may see specific things about the life being imitated and about our own lives. As William Faulkner put it, "Art is simpler than people think because there is so little to write about. All the moving things are eternal in man's history and have been written before."[13]

All of which leads to the question of value that I raised early in this study, a question that turns on another: What is the purpose of narrative art? Surely Tomashevsky and the other Russian formalists are correct in their contention that what art does is "defamiliarize"—or more simply, reorder—selected elements of life so that we can resee them—that is, really see them. Perhaps this, as well as the views of Jameson, Hartman, and Sacks that I cited earlier, can be summed up in Conrad's famous declaration of his fictional intent: to make us *see*. Ross Macdonald at his best—in *The Ivory Grin, The Doomsters, The Zebra-Striped Hearse, Black Money, The Goodbye Look, The Underground*

Man—makes us see what all valuable fiction makes us see: old things, things we have seen before, things we know go into making the human creature what he is, things we know so well that we forget them until we read a Lew Archer novel.

Of the many descriptions of what Macdonald's novels make us see anew and understand more deeply, George Grella's is the most accurate and eloquent: "All men are guilty and all human actions are connected. The past is never past. The child is father to the man. True reality resides in dreams. And most of all, everyone gets what he deserves, but no one deserves what he gets."[14]

Notes and References

Preface

1. L. L. Lee, "The Art of Ross Macdonald," *South Dakota Review* 24 (Spring 1986): 55–67.

2. John Leonard, "Ross Macdonald, His Lew Archer and Other Secret Selves," *New York Times Book Review,* 1 June 1969, 2.

3. Peter Wolfe, *Dreamers Who Live Their Dreams: The World of Ross Macdonald's Novels* (Bowling Green, Ohio: Bowling Green State University Popular Press, 1976), 21.

Chapter One

1. *Self-Portrait: Ceaselessly into the Past* (Santa Barbara: Capra Press, 1981), 15; hereafter cited in the text as *SP.*

2. Matthew J. Bruccoli, *Ross Macdonald* (New York: Harcourt Brace Jovanovich, 1984), 3.

3. Robert Easton, "A Quiet Man," in *Inward Journey: Ross Macdonald,* ed. Ralph B. Sipper (New York: Mysterious Press, 1987), 49.

4. Macdonald mentioned this incident himself (*SP,*40), but see also Bruccoli, *Ross Macdonald,* and Easton, "A Quiet Man."

5. Quoted in Paul Nelson, "It's All One Case," in Sipper, *Inward Journey,* 68.

6. Raymond A. Sokoloff, "The Art of Murder," *Newsweek,* 22 March 1971, 106.

7. Jerry Tutunjian, "A Conversation with Ross Macdonald," *Tamarack Review* 62 (1974): 68.

8. Leonard, "Ross Macdonald," 2.

9. Sokoloff, "The Art of Murder," 106.

10. Leonard, "Ross Macdonald," 2.

11. Bruccoli, for example, cites the following: "I was a rebel in most respects; I used to take incredible risks," as well as Macdonald's statement that he "narrowly escaped becoming a criminal." Bruccoli, *Ross Macdonald,* 6.

12. Easton, "A Quiet Man," 45.

13. Ibid., 49–50.

14. Margaret Millar, "Highlights," in Sipper, *Inward Journey,* 43.

15. Gene Davidson and John Knoerle, "Ross Macdonald Interview," *Mystery* (November/December 1979), 9; quoted in Bruccoli, *Ross Macdonald,* 11–12.

16. Letter to Ivan von Auw, 12 September 1948, copy at Humanities Research Center, University of Texas; quoted in Bruccoli, *Ross Macdonald,* 28.

17. Ibid.

18. Ibid., 78.

19. Letter to Alfred A. Knopf, 9 March 1958, Knopf Papers, Humanities Research Center, University of Texas; quoted in Bruccoli, *Ross Macdonald,* 59.

20. Letter to Ivan von Auw, 27 May 1957, Princeton University Library; quoted in Bruccoli, *Ross Macdonald,* 55.

21. John Leonard, "I Care Who Killed Roger Ackroyd," *Esquire,* August 1975, 60–61, 120.

22. William Goldman, "The Goodbye Look," *New York Times Book Review,* 1 June 1969, 1.

23. Leonard, "Ross Macdonald," 2.

24. Wayne Warga, "The Millars: Tale of Fortitude," *Los Angeles Times,* 11 February 1982, 1.

25. Ibid., 26.

26. Julian Symonds, "A Transatlantic Friendship," in Sipper, *Inward Journey,* 65.

27. Warga, "Tale of Fortitude," 26.

28. Ibid.

29. Wolfe, *Dreamers,* 21.

30. Bruccoli, *Ross Macdonald,* 72.

31. Tutunjian, "Conversation," 73.

32. Jon Carroll, "Ross Macdonald in Raw California," *Esquire,* June 1972, 149.

33. *The Blue Hammer* (New York: Alfred A. Knopf, 1976), 79.

34. Sam Grogg, Jr., "Ross Macdonald: At the Edge," *Journal of Popular Culture* (Summer 73), 222.

35. Ibid.

36. Ibid, 219.

37. Steven R. Carter, "Ross Macdonald: The Complexity of the Modern Quest for Justice," in *Mystery & Detection Annual,* 1973, ed. Donald K. Adams (Beverly Hills: Donald Adams, 1974), 59.

38. Edward Margolies, *Which Way Did He Go? The Private Eye in Dashiell Hammett, Raymond Chandler, Chester Himes, and Ross Macdonald* (New York: Holmet Meirn, 1982), 80.

39. Grogg, "At the Edge," 218.

40. Jacques Barzun, "Ross Macdonald: *The Drowning Pool,*" in *A Book of Prefaces* (New York: Garlent, 1976), 77.

41. Tutunjian, "Conversation," 85.

42. Carroll, "Raw California," 149.

43. Grogg, "At the Edge," 216.

44. Carroll, "Raw California," 149.

45. Grogg, "At the Edge," 222.

Chapter Two

1. Eudora Welty, "The Stuff That Nightmares Are Made Of," *New York Times Book Review,* 14 February 1971, 1, 29.

2. Walter Clemons, "Ross Macdonald at His Best," *New York Times,* 19 February 1971, 33.

3. Sokoloff, "The Art of Murder," 102.

4. Richard Schickel, "Detective Story," *Commentary,* September 1971, 96.

5. Bruce Cook, "Ross Macdonald: The Prince in the Poorhouse," *Catholic World,* October 1971, 30.

6. G. A. Finch, "The Case of the Underground Man: Evolution or Devolution," *Armchair Detective* 6 (August 1973): 210.

7. Geoffrey Hartman, "Literature High and Low," in *The Fate of Reading and Other Essays* (Chicago: University of Chicago Press, 1975), 218.

8. T. R. Steiner, "The Mind of the Hardboiled: Ross Macdonald and the Roles of Criticism," *South Dakota Review* 24 (Spring 86): 44.

9. Sokoloff, "The Art of Murder," 101.

10. See especially *Modern Fiction Studies* 29 (Autumn 83) and *South Dakota Review* 24 (Spring 86).

11. E. D. Hirsch, Jr., *Validity in Interpretation* (New Haven: Yale University Press, 1967), 98.

12. Glenn W. Most and William W. Stowe, eds., *The Poetics of Murder: Detective Fiction and Literary Theory* (New York: Harcourt Brace Jovanovich, 1983).

13. Zahava K. Dorinson, "Ross Macdonald: The Personal Paradigm and Popular Fiction," *Armchair Detective* 10 (1977): 43.

14. The most notorious of these are S. S. Van Dine, "Twenty Rules for Writing Detective Stories," and Ronald A. Knox, "Detective Story Decalogue," collected with the amusing and not totally ironic "The Detection Club Oath" under the rubric "The Rules of the Game" in *The Art of the Mystery Story,* ed. Howard Haycraft (New York: Biblo and Tannen, 1976), 189–99.

15. Keith Newlin, "C. W. Sughrue's Whiskey Visions," *Modern Fiction Studies* 29 (Autumn 1983): 546.

16. Finch, "The Underground Man," 211.

17. John G. Cawelti, *Adventure, Mystery, and Romance: Formula Stories as Art and Popular Culture* (Chicago: University of Chicago Press, 1976), and George Grella, "Murder and the Mean Streets: The Hardboiled Detective Novel," in *Detective Fiction: Crime and Compromise,* ed. Dick Allen and David Chacko (New York: Harcourt Brace Jovanovich, 1974), 411–28.

18. Timothy Steele, "The Structure of the Detective Story: Classical or Modern? *Modern Fiction Studies* 27 (Winter 1981–1982): 562.

19. Quoted in "A Catalogue of Crime," in *A Collection of Reviews* (Northridge: Lord John Press, 1979), 8.

20. Steele, "Structure of the Detective Story," 557.

21. Ibid., 559.

22. Dorothy Gardiner and Katherine Sorley Walker, eds., *Raymond Chandler Speaking* (Boston: Houghton Mifflin, 1977), 63–64.

23. Joseph E. Shaw, Introduction, *Early Stories from "Black Mask," The Hardboiled Omnibus* (New York: Simon and Schuster, 1946), vi.

24. F. R. Leavis, *The Great Tradition* (New York: New York University Press, 1963), 2.

25. Cawelti, *Adventure, Mystery, and Romance*, 139.

26. Ibid., 142.

27. Grella, "Murder and the Mean Streets," 442.

28. Ibid., 414.

29. Ibid.

30. Cawelti, *Adventure, Mystery, and Romance*, 142.

31. One of the clearest expositions of this position is Nina Baym, "Melodramas of Beset Manhood: How Theories of American Literature Exclude Women Authors," in *The New Feminist Criticism: Essays on Women, Literature, and Theory*, ed. Elaine Showalter, (New York: Random House, 1985), 63–79. For a more extreme view, see Judith Fetterly, *The Resisting Reader: A Feminist Approach to American Fiction* (Bloomington: Indiana University Press, 1978).

32. Baym, "Melodramas of Beset Manhood," 71.

33. Ibid., 72.

34. Geoffrey O'Brien, *Hardboiled America: The Lurid Years of Paperbacks* (New York: Van Nostrand Reinhold Company, 1981), 5.

35. "The Detective in Fiction," in *A Collection of Reviews*, 1.

36. Gilbert Sorrentino, "Ross Macdonald: Some Remarks on the Limitation of Form," in Sipper, *Inward Journey*, 148.

37. Warga, "Tale of Fortitude," 26.

38. Most and Stowe, *Poetics of Murder*, xi.

39. Michael Holquist, "Whodunit and Other Questions," in Most and Stowe, *Poetics of Murder*, 152.

40. See Edmund Wilson, "Why Do People Read Detective Stories?" and "Who Cares Who Killed Roger Ackroyd?" in *Classics and Commercials: A Literary Chronicle of the Forties* (New York: Random House, 1962), 231–37 and 257–65.

41. David I. Grossvogel, "Agatha Christie: Containment of the Unknown," in Most and Stowe, *Poetics of Murder*, 252–65.

42. Hartman's assertion that neither Chandler nor Macdonald "puts much emphasis on problem solving" is typical.

43. Cawelti, *Adventure, Mystery, and Romance*, 159.

44. Mickey Spillane, *I, the Jury* (New York: E.P. Dutton, 1948), 173.

45. Hartman, "Literature High and Low," 212.

46. Frank Kermode, "Novel and Narrative," in Most and Stowe, *Poetics of Murder*, 180.

47. Most and Stowe, *Poeteics of Murder*, xxi.

48. Hartman, "Literature High and Low," 212.

49. For a discussion of how preconceived notions about a work's popular or serious status alters both reading and interpretation, see Peter Rabinowitz, *Before Reading: Narrative Conventions and the Politics of Interpretation* (Ithaca, N.Y.: Cornell University Press, 1987), 183–93.

50. Terry Eagleton, *Literary Theory,* (Minneapolis: University of Minnesota Press, 1983), 9.

51. Ibid., 14.

52. Frederic Jameson, "On Raymond Chandler," in Most and Stowe, *Poetics of Murder,* 125.

53. Hartman, "Literature High and Low," 210.

54. Sheldon Sacks, "The Pursuit of Lew Archer," *Critical Inquiry* 6 (Winter 79): 232.

Chapter Three

1. Wolfe, *Dreamers,* 68.

2. *The Dark Tunnel* (New York: Dodd, Mead, 1944), 9; hereafter cited in the text.

3. *Trouble Follows Me* (New York: Dutton, 1946), 70; hereafter cited in the text.

4. Letter to Alfred A. Knopf, published as "Farewell, Chandler" in Sipper, *Inward Journey,* 38.

5. *Blue City,* (New York: Alfred A. Knopf, 1947), 12; hereafter cited in the text.

6. "Mystery and Crime," *New Yorker,* 23 August 1947, 80.

7. Wolfe, *Dreamers,* 100.

8. *The Three Roads* (New York: Alfred A. Knopf, 1948), 29; hereafter cited in the text.

9. Jerry Speir, *Ross Macdonald* (New York: Frederick Unger, 1978), 24.

10. *The Moving Target* (New York: Alfred A. Knopf, 1949), 9; hereafter cited in the text.

11. Quoted in Carter, "Modern Quest for Justice," 69.

12. Daniel Barnes, " 'I'm The Eye': Archer as Narrator in the Novels of Ross Macdonald," *Mystery & Detection Annual,* 1972, ed. Donald K. Adams (Beverly Hills: Donald Adams, 1973), 179.

13. Tutunjian, "Conversation," 81.

14. Ibid.

15. Ibid.

16. *The Far Side of the Dollar* (New York: Alfred A. Knopf, 1969), 175.

Chapter Four

1. "Farewell, Chandler," 40.

2. *The Drowning Pool* (New York: Alfred A. Knopf, 1950), 7; hereafter cited in the text.

3. *The Way Some People Die* (New York: Alfred A. Knopf, 1951), 9; hereafter cited in the text.

4. *The Ivory Grin* (New York: Alfred A. Knopf, 1952), 111; hereafter cited in the text.

5. Letter to Alfred A. Knopf, 28 August 1952; quoted in Bruccoli, *Ross Macdonald,* 49.

6. Hugh Kenner, "Learning," in Sipper, *Inward Journey,* 58.

7. "Farewell Chandler," 37–42.

8. Anthony Boucher, "Criminals at Large," *New York Times Book Review,* 1 August 1954, 15.

9. Wolfe, *Dreamers,* 146.

10. Speir, *Ross Macdonald,* 37.

11. *Find A Victim* (New York: Alfred A. Knopf, 1954), 161; hereafter cited in the text.

12. Wolfe, *Dreamers,* 153.

13. *The Barbarous Coast* (New York: Alfred A. Knopf, 1956), 3; hereafter cited in the text.

Chapter Five

1. Quoted in Bruccoli, *Ross Macdonald,* 56.

2. Sheldon Sacks, *Fiction and the Shape of Belief* (Berkeley: University of California Press, 1966), 15.

3. *The Doomsters* (New York: Alfred A. Knopf, 1958), 36; hereafter cited in the text.

4. Clifford A. Ridley, "Yes, Most of My Chronicles Are Chronicles of Misfortune," *National Observer,* 31 July 1976, 17.

5. Jerry Speir, "Writing *Ross Macdonald,*" in Sipper, *Inward Journey,* 93.

Chapter Six

1. Bruccoli, *Ross Macdonald,* 56, suggests that Macdonald himself may have written the flap copy.

2. Margolies, *Which Way Did He Go?* 80.

3. *The Galton Case* (New York: Alfred A. Knopf, 1959), 237; hereafter cited in the text.

4. Bruccoli, *Ross Macdonald,* 81.

5. *The Wycherly Woman* (New York: Alfred A. Knopf, 1961), 9; hereafter cited in the text.

6. Speir, *Ross Macdonald,* 60.

7. *The Zebra-Striped Hearse* (New York: Alfred A. Knopf, 1962), 258; hereafter cited in the text.

8. Wilfrid Sheed, "The Good Word," *New York Times Book Review,* 5 September 1971, 2.

9. Speir, *Ross Macdonald,* 78.
10. Wolfe, *Dreamers,* 232–33.
11. Steiner, "Mind of the Hardboiled," 44.

Chapter Seven

1. *The Instant Enemy* (New York: Alfred A. Knopf, 1968), 133; hereafter cited in the text.
2. *Black Money* (New York: Alfred A. Knopf, 1966), 9; hereafter cited in the text.
3. R. S. Crane, "The Concept of Plot and the Plot of *Tom Jones,*" in *Critics and Criticism: Essays in Method by a Group of Chicago Critics,* ed. R. S. Crane (Chicago: University of Chicago Press, 1957), 67.
4. Leonard, "Ross Macdonald," 19.
5. Margolies, *Which Way Did He Go?* 82.
6. F. Scott Fitzgerald, *The Great Gatsby,* Scribner's Classic Edition (New York: Charles Scribner's Sons, 1925), 48.
7. Steiner, "The Mind of the Hardboiled," 31.
8. Ibid., 42.
9. Ibid., 40.

Chapter Eight

1. Letter to Ashbel Green, 19 July 1970; quoted in Bruccoli, *Ross Macdonald,* 101.
2. Speir, *Ross Macdonald,* 102.
3. *The Underground Man,* (New York: Alfred A. Knopf, 1971), 3; hereafter cited in the text.
4. Goldman, "The Goodbye Look," 2.
5. Cook, "The Prince in the Poorhouse," 30.
6. Speir, *Ross Macdonald,* 104.
7. Hartman, "Literature High and Low," 221–22.
8. Ibid., 214.

Chapter Nine

1. Speir, *Ross Macdonald,* 104.
2. Wolfe, *Dreamers,* 333.
3. Crawford Woods, "The Sleeping Beauty," *New York Times Book Review,* 20 May 1973, 55.
4. Ibid.
5. Bruccoli, *Ross Macdonald,* 108.
6. Ibid., 112.
7. Sacks, "The Pursuit of Lew Archer," 233.
8. Leavis, *The Great Tradition,* 2.

9. Robert B. Parker, "Heroes and Debts," in Sipper, *Inward Journey,* 137.

10. Dennis Lynds, "Expanding the *Roman Noir:* Ross Macdonald's Legacy to Mystery/Detective Authors," *South Dakota Review* 24 (Spring 86): 123–24.

11. George Grella, "Evil Plots," *New Republic,* 26 July 1975, 24.

12. L. L. Lee, "The Art of Ross Macdonald," 65.

13. Joseph Blotner, ed., *Selected Letters of William Faulkner* (New York: Random House, 1977), 185–86.

14. Grella, "Evil Plots," 26.

Selected Bibliography

PRIMARY WORKS

Novels

The Barbarous Coast. New York: Alfred A. Knopf, 1956.
Black Money. New York: Alfred A. Knopf, 1966.
Blue City. New York; Alfred A. Knopf, 1947.
The Blue Hammer. New York: Alfred A. Knopf, 1976.
The Chill. New York: Alfred A. Knopf, 1964.
The Dark Tunnel. New York: Dodd, Mead, 1944.
The Doomsters. New York: Alfred A. Knopf, 1958.
The Drowning Pool. New York: Alfred A. Knopf, 1950.
The Far Side of the Dollar. New York: Alfred A. Knopf, 1965.
The Ferguson Affair. New York: Alfred A. Knopf, 1960.
Find a Victim. New York: Alfred A. Knopf, 1954.
The Galton Case. New York: Alfred A. Knopf, 1959.
The Goodbye Look. New York: Alfred A. Knopf, 1969.
The Instant Enemy. New York: Alfred A. Knopf, 1968.
The Ivory Grin. New York: Alfred A. Knopf, 1952.
Meet Me at the Morgue. New York: Alfred A. Knopf, 1953.
The Moving Target. New York: Alfred A. Knopf, 1949.
Sleeping Beauty. New York: Alfred A. Knopf, 1973.
The Three Roads. New York: Alfred A. Knopf, 1949.
Trouble Follows Me. New York: Dodd, Mead, 1946.
The Underground Man. New York: Alfred A. Knopf, 1971.
The Way Some People Die. New York: Alfred A. Knopf, 1951.
The Wycherly Woman. New York: Alfred A. Knopf, 1961.
The Zebra-Striped Hearse. New York: Alfred A. Knopf, 1962.

Collected Short Stories

Lew Archer, Private Detective. New York: Mysterious Press, 1977.
The Name is Archer. New York: Bantam, 1955.

Collected Novels

Archer at Large (The Galton Case, The Chill, Black Money). New York: Alfred A. Knopf, 1970.

Archer in Hollywood (The Moving Target, The Way Some People Die, The Barbarous Coast). New York: Alfred A. Knopf, 1967.
Archer in Jeopardy (The Doomsters, The Zebra-Striped Hearse, The Instant Enemy). New York, Alfred A. Knopf, 1979.

Collected Nonfiction

A Collection of Reviews. Northridge: Lord John Press, 1979.
Early Millar. Santa Barbara: Cordelia Editions, 1982. Juvenilia of Margaret and Kenneth Millar.
Great Stories of Suspense (editor). New York: Alfred A. Knopf, 1974.
On Crime Writing. Santa Barbara: Capra Press, 1973.
Self-Portrait: Ceaselessly into the Past. Edited by Ralph B. Sipper. Santa Barbara: Capra Press, 1981. Interviews and occasional pieces.

SECONDARY WORKS

Interviews

"A Conversation with the Author." *Santa Barbara News & Review*, 23 March 1973, 7.
Carroll, Jon, "Ross Macdonald in Raw California." *Esquire*, June 1972, 148–49, 188.
Cooper-Clark, Dianna. "Interview with Ross Macdonald." In *Designs of Darkness*. Bowling Green, Ohio: Bowling Green State University Popular Press, 1983, 83–100.
Darrach, Brad. "Ross Macdonald: The Man Behind the Mysteries." *People*, 8 July 1974, 26–30.
Grogg, Sam, Jr. "Ross Macdonald: At the Edge." *Journal of Popular Culture* 7 (Summer 1973): 213–22.
Leonard, John. "Ross Macdonald, His Lew Archer and Other Secret Selves." *New York Times Book Review*, 1 June 1969, 2, 19.
Ridley, Clifford A. "Yes, Most of My Chronicles Are Chronicles of Misfortune." *National Observer*, 31 July 1976, 17.
Tutunjian, Jerry. "A Conversation with Ross Macdonald." *Tamarack Review* 62 (1974): 66–85.

Bibliography

Bruccoli, Matthew J. *Kenneth Millar/Ross Macdonald: A Descriptive Bibliography*. Pittsburgh: University of Pittsburgh Press, 1983.

Books and Articles That Discuss the American Detective Novel

Babener, Liahna K. "California Babylon: The World of American Detective Fiction." *Clues* 1 (1980): 77–89. A sound assessment of the use of California and 'the American dream' in the hardboiled novel.

Beekman, E. M. "Raymond Chandler and an American Genre." *Massachusetts Review* 14 (1973): 149–57. A good if incomplete attempt to define the American detective novel as a genre.

Byrd, Max. "The Detective Detected: From Sophocles to Ross Macdonald." *Yale Review* 64 (1974): 72–83. Some quite interesting, and also some quite misguided, remarks on detective fiction and Macdonald's work.

Cawelti, John G. *Adventure, Mystery, and Romance: Formula Stories as Art and Popular Culture.* Chicago: University of Chicago Press, 1976. Easily the most influential study of formula fiction in general and detective fiction in particular.

French, Warren. "William Faulkner and the Art of the Detective Story." In *The Thirties: Fiction, Poetry, Drama,* edited by Warren French, 55–62. Deland, Florida: Everett/Edwards, 1975. Discusses Faulkner's use of the techniques of detective fiction in his early novels, and sees that "the genre appears trivial only because it has attracted so many hack writers."

Geherin, David. *The American Private Eye: The Image in Fiction.* New York, Frederick Ungar, 1985. Brief accounts of the major and minor private eyes and their authors. Section on Macdonald headed "The Compassionate Eye."

Grella, George. "Murder and the Mean Streets: The Hardboiled Detective Novel." In *Detective Fiction: Crime and Compromise,* edited by Dick Allen and David Chacko, 411–28. New York: Harcourt Brace Jovanovich, 1974. Intelligent and informed discussion of the hardboiled genre. Still important.

Grimes, Larry E. "Stepsons of Sam: Re-visions of the Hardboiled Detective Formula in Recent American Fiction." *Modern Fiction Studies* 29 (Autumn 1983): 535–56. Views novels by Jules Pfeiffer, Richard Brautigan, and Thomas Berger as "re-visions" of the Cawelti formula.

Jameson, Fredric. "On Raymond Chandler." *The Southern Review* 6 (1970): 624–50. An often brilliant meditation on things American—society, politics, literature, language, and detective novels.

Mahan, Jeffrey. "The Hardboiled Detective in the Fallen World." *Clues* 1 (Fall/Winter, 1980): 90–99. Evaluates the moral world of the American detective novel according to concepts from Reinhold Niebuhr and Karl Barth. Strains in places.

Margolies, Edward. *Which Way Did He Go? The Private Eye in Dashiell Hammett, Raymond Chandler, Chester Himes, and Ross Macdonald.* New York: Holmes and Meier, 1982. Good chapter on Macdonald.

Most, Glenn W. and William W. Stowe, eds. *The Poetics of Murder: Detective Fiction and Literary Theory.* New York: Harcourt Brace Jovanovich, 1983. A collection of essays and excerpts, the primary interest of which is literary theory rather than detective fiction.

O'Brien, Geoffrey. *Hardboiled America: The Lurid Years of Paperbacks.* New York: Van Nostrand Reinhold, 1981. An interesting and often entertaining discussion of the art of the paperback covers of hardboiled fiction, and a sensible assessment of the fiction between those covers as well.

Paterson, John. "A Cosmic View of the Private Eye." *Saturday Review,* 22 August 1953, 7–8, 31–33. Still one of the best general discussions of the genre.

Porter, Joseph C. "The End of the Trail: The American West of Dashiell Hammett and Raymond Chandler." *Western Historical Quarterly* 6 (October 1975): 411–24. Sees the form as a "modernization" of the western, the subject of which is the American West.

Ruehlman, William. *Saint with a Gun: The Unlawful Private Eye.* New York: New York University Press, 1974. The private eye as "the most modern of American heroes . . . half saint and half headsman."

Stade, George. "I've Been Reading Thrillers." *Columbia Forum* (Spring 1970): 34–37. Sensible discussion of the nature of popular literature—"literature read in a certain way."

Steele, Timothy. "The Structure of the Detective Story: Classical or Modern?" *Modern Fiction Studies* 27 (Winter 1981–1982): 555–70. Indispensable for anyone who would speak intelligently about plots in detective or any other kind of fiction.

Svoboda, Frederic. "The Snub-nosed Mystique: Observations on the American Detective Hero." *Modern Fiction Studies* 29 (Autumn 1983): 557–68. Sees the American private detective as the contemporary "gunfighter" on the "moral frontier," and as "the messiah of order."

Van Meter, Jan R. "Sophocles and the Rest of the Boys in the Pulps: Myth and the Detective Novel." In *Dimensions of Detective Fiction,* edited by Larry N. Landrum, Pat Browne, and Ray B. Browne, 12–21. Bowling Green, Ohio: Bowling Green State University Press, 1976. Discusses the ritualistic aspect of detective novels, emphasizing that they, like myth, often "embody" reality without "explaining" it.

Winks, Robin W. *Modus Operandi: An Excursion into Detective Fiction.* Boston: David R. Godine, 1982. Comments on all forms of detective fiction.

Books and Articles about Macdonald and His Work

Barnes, Daniel R. " 'I'm The Eye': Archer as Narrator in the Novels of Ross Macdonald." In *Mystery and Detection Annual,* 1972, edited by Donald K. Adams, 178–90. Beverly Hills: Donald Adams, 1972. Makes preliminary inquiries into the epistomological questions raised by the novels, then concentrates on "eye" imagery.

Bruccoli, Matthew J. *Ross Macdonald.* New York: Harcourt Brace Jovanovich, 1984. Valuable critical biography.

Busch, Susan Runholt. "Ross Macdonald as Chronicler of Southern California." *South Dakota Review* 24 (Spring, 1986): 111–20.

Carter, Steven R. "Ross Macdonald: The Complexity of the Modern Quest for Justice." In *Mystery and Detection Annual,* 1973, edited by Donald K. Adams, 59–82. Beverly Hills: Donald Adams, 1973. Relates justice to psychology, but sometimes finds justice in the imagined events following the novels. Contains important citations from letter of Macdonald to the author.

Coombs, William W. "The Detective as Both Tortoise and Achilles: Archer Gets the Feel of the Case in *The Chill.*" *Clues* 2 (Spring/Summer 1981): 98–105. The relevance of the allusions to Zeno's paradoxes and pre-Socratic philosophy in the novel.

Dorinson, Zahava K. "Ross Macdonald: The Personal Paradigm and Popular Fiction." *Armchair Detective* 10 (1977): 43–45, 87. Assesses Macdonald according to the "formula" of the hunt.

Easton, Robert. "A Quiet Man." In *Inward Journey: Ross Macdonald,* edited by Ralph B. Sipper, 45–54. New York: Mysterious Press, 1987. Personal appreciation of Ken Millar.

Finch, G. A. "The Case of *The Underground Man:* Evolution or Devolution." *Armchair Detective* 8 (1972/73): 210–12. Good example of what results when a critic attempts to evaluate a generic novel according to arbitrary formulaic "rules."

Fishman, Charles. "Another Peacock Cry: Heraldic Birds in Five Lew Archer Novels." *Clues* 2 (Spring/Summer, 1981) 106–115.

Geherin, David. "Archer in Hollywood: The Barbarous Coast of Ross Macdonald." *Armchair Detective* 9 (1975/1976): 55–58. Macdonald's use of Hollywood in his fiction is not "profound" but "skillful" and "inevitable."

Grella, George. "Evil Plots." *New Republic,* 26 July 75, 24–26. The best general essay on the Archer novels.

Hartman, Geoffrey. "Literature High and Low: the Case of the Mystery Story." In *The Fate of Reading and Other Essays,* 203–22. Chicago: University of Chicago Press, 1975. Argues that detective novels can't be "high literature."

Holton, Judith, and Orley I. Holton. "The Time-Space Dimension in the Lew Archer Detective Novels." *North Dakota Quarterly* (Autumn 1972): 30–41. Somehow, because Archer travels a lot and the novels deal with events in the past, they argue that "man can not escape or remake what he is but must learn to cope with it."

Kenner, Hugh. "Learning." In *Inward Journey: Ross Macdonald,* ed. Ralph B. Sipper, 55–58. New York: Mysterious Press, 1987. Memoir.

Lee, L. L. "The Art of Ross Macdonald." *South Dakota Review* 24 (Spring 1986): 55–67. Account of the attitudes—"marxisant" and otherwise—that he finds implicit in Macdonald's work.

Lynds, Dennis. "Expanding the *Roman Noir*: Ross Macdonald's Legacy to Mystery/Detective Authors." *South Dakota Review* 24 (Spring 1986): 121–24.

Pry, Elmer B. "Ross Macdonald's Violent California: Imagery Patterns in *The*

Underground Man." *Western American Literature* 9 (Fall 1974): 197–203. Good analysis of the function of images in the novel.

_____. "Lew Archer's 'Moral Landscape.'" *Armchair Detective* 8 (1974/75) 174–81. A clear and coherent expression of the accepted view of Archer's morality—a view that needs qualification.

Sacks, Sheldon. "The Pursuit of Lew Archer." *Critical Inquiry* 6 (Winter 1979): 231–38. Argues correctly that Macdonald's value lies not in his works being something better than detective novels but instead in their being excellent detective novels.

Sipper, Ralph B., ed. *Inward Journey: Ross Macdonald.* New York: Mysterious Press, 1987. Valuable collection of appreciations of Ross Macdonald and his work by his friends; includes "The Scene of the Crime," a paper Macdonald read on radio in 1954, and, under the title "Farewell, Chandler," Macdonald's "manifesto" letter to his editor.

Skenazy, Paul. "Bring It All Back Home: Ross Macdonald's California." *South Dakota Review* 24 (Spring, 1986): 68–110. A somewhat subjective view of Macdonald's work.

Sorrentino, Gilbert. "Ross Madonald: Some Remarks on the Limitations of Form." In *Inward Journey: Ross Macdonald,* ed. Ralph B. Sipper, 148–53. New York: Mysterious Press, 1987. Agrees with Sacks, but sees more "limitations" in the genre than perhaps exist.

Speir, Jerry. *Ross Macdonald.* New York: Frederick Unger, 1978. Good introduction to Macdonald's work.

_____. "Writing *Ross Macdonald.*" In *Inward Journey: Ross Macdonald,* ed. Ralph B. Sipper, 89–94. New York: Mysterious Press, 1987. Recounts his discussion with Macdonald when working on the Ungar book; especially amusing is Speir's account of his attempt to get Macdonald to discuss the "ideas" in his novels.

Steiner, T. R. "The Mind of the Hardboiled: Ross Macdonald and the Roles of Criticism." *South Dakota Review* 24 (Spring 1986): 29–54. One of the best discussions of Macdonald's work.

Symonds, Julian. "A Transatlantic Friendship." In *Inward Journey: Ross Macdonald,* ed. Ralph B. Sipper, 59–66. New York: Mysterious Press, 1987.

Wolfe, Peter. *Dreamers Who Live Their Dreams: The World of Ross Macdonald.* Bowling Green, Ohio: Bowling Green State University Popular Press, 1976. First book-length study of Macdonald and his fiction.

Young, Noel. "His Silent Smile." In *Inward Journey: Ross Macdonald,* ed. Ralph B. Sipper, 80–82. New York: Mysterious Press, 1987.

Index

Aristotle, 23
Auden, W. H., 7

Babener, Liahna K., 143
Barnes, Daniel, 45, 144
Barzun, Jacques, 16, 22
Baym, Nina, 26, 136
Beekman, E. M., 143
Bellow, Saul, 27
Big Sleep, The (Raymond Chandler), 29
Bloom, Harold, 63
Bogart, Humphrey, 28
Boucher, Anthony, 10, 63
Brand, Max, 126
Bruccoli, Matthew, 1, 2, 10, 13, 89, 96, 127, 133, 142, 144
Busch, Susan Runholt, 144
Byrd, Max, 143

Carroll, Jon, 142
Carter, Stephen R., 145
Catullus, 16
Cawelti, John, 22, 24, 25, 32, 143
Chandler, Raymond, 9, 10, 11, 22, 23, 45, 46, 50, 51, 62, 63, 66, 99, 100, 130
Christie, Agatha, 22, 23
Clemons, Walter, 20
Conrad, Joseph, 130
Cook, Bruce, 20, 120
Coombs, William W., 145
Cooper, James Fenimore, 24
Cooper-Clark, Dianna, 142
Crane, R. S., 101
Crane, Stephen, 24, 35, 37
Crumley, James, 27

Darrach, Brad, 142
Dickens, Charles, 21
Didion, Joan, 17
Dorinson, Zahava K., 145
Doyle, Arthur Conan, 24, 27

Eagleton, Terry, 23
Easton, Robert, 6, 145

Farewell, My Lovely (Raymond Chandler), 32, 59
Faulkner, William, 21, 130
Finch, G. A., 20, 145
Fishman, Charles, 145
Fitzgerald, F. Scott, 24, 100, 105
Fleming, Ian, 22
French, Warren, 143
Freud, Sigmund, 14–15

Gardner, Erle Stanley, 126
Geherin, David, 143, 145
Goldman, William, 11, 120
Great Gatsby, The (F. Scott Fitzgerald), 102
Grella, George, 22, 24–25, 129, 131, 143, 145
Greenleaf, Stephen, 28
Grimes, Larry E., 143
Grogg, Sam Jr., 142
Grossvogel, David, 30

Hammett, Dashiell, 9, 10, 11, 23, 24, 27, 45, 99, 100
Hardy, Thomas, 21, 75
Harper (film), 10, 11
Hartman, Geoffrey, 20, 32, 33, 125, 130, 145
Heart of Darkness (Joseph Conrad), 26
Hemingway, Ernest, 24, 100
Hirsch, E. D., Jr., 21
Holquist, Michael, 29, 31
Holton, Judith and Orley I., 145
Huxley, Aldous, 17

I, The Jury (Mickey Spillane), 31

Jameson, Fredric, 33, 130, 143

Kenner, Hugh, 61, 145

Kermode, Frank, 32

Lady Chatterly's Lover (D. H. Lawrence), 40
Lawrence, D. H., 42
Leavis, F. R., 23, 128
le Carré, John, 21
Lee, L. L., 130, 142
Les Miserables, 21
Little Drummer Girl, The (John le Carré), 21
Long Goodbye, The (Raymond Chandler), 32, 69
Lynds, Dennis, 128, 129, 145

MacDonald, John D., 9, 28
Macdonald, Ross

  WORKS:
  Barbarous Coast, The, 9, 51, 66–68
  Black Money, 10, 99, 100, 102–105, 109, 130
  Blue City, 7, 25, 38, 39, 105
  Blue Hammer, The, 12, 83, 126, 127–28
  Chill, The, 10, 93–94
  Dark Tunnel, The, 7, 35–37, 38
  Doomsters, The, 9, 10, 69–82, 130
  Drowning Pool, The, 9, 12, 13, 51–54
  Far Side of the Dollar, The, 10, 49, 93, 94–98
  Ferguson Affair, The, 10, 16, 88–89
  Find a Victim, 9, 63–66, 94
  "Find the Woman," 7
  Galton Case, The, 3, 5, 9, 10, 11, 13, 81, 83–88, 97, 99
  Goodbye Look, The, 11, 12, 99, 100, 109–13, 114, 130
  Instant Enemy, The, 10, 99, 100, 101, 105–109
  Ivory Grin, The, 9, 54, 55–61, 68, 130
  Meet Me at the Morgue, 61–62
  Moving Target, The, 8, 10, 35, 42, 43, 44, 47–50, 51
  Sleeping Beauty, 12, 16, 126–27
  Three Roads, The, 8, 35, 38, 40–42
  Trouble Follows Me, 7, 35, 37–38

Underground Man, The, 11, 12, 20, 32, 114–26, 130
Way Some People Die, The, 9, 54–55, 68
Wycherly Woman, The, 10, 89–90, 100
Zebra-Striped Hearse, The, 11, 15, 91–93, 130

Mahan, Jeffrey, 143
Mailer, Norman, 27
Maltese Falcon, The, 6, 28, 31–32, 38
Margolies, Edward, 15, 84, 143
Millar, Anne, 2, 4, 5, 83
Millar, Beth, 3
Millar, John, 2, 3, 4, 83
Millar, Kenneth. See Macdonald, Ross
Millar, Linda, 7, 9, 10, 13
Millar, Margaret Sturm, 6, 7, 9, 10, 12, 13
Millar, Rob, 3
Mitchum, Robert, 28
Most, Glenn W., 143

Newman, Paul, 10, 12
No Exit, (John-Paul Sartre), 95

O'Brien, Geoffrey, 27, 144
Oliver Twist (Charles Dickens), 5

Parker, Robert B., 18, 128
Parrington, Vernon, 36
Paterson, John, 144
Peanuts (Charles Schultz), 23, 28
Poe, Edgar Allan, 22
Poirier, Richard, 26
Porter, Joseph C., 144
Pry, Elmer B., 145–46
Pynchon, Thomas, 17

Rabinowitz, Peter, 137n49
Red Harvest (Dashiell Hammett), 39
Reuhlman, William, 144
Ridley, Clifford A., 142

Sacks, Sheldon, 33, 128, 130, 146
Sayers, Dorothy, 22
Schickel, Richard, 20
Shaw, Joseph, 23
Sheed, Wilfred, 93, 98
Sipper, Ralph B., 146

Skenazy, Paul, 146
Sokoloff, Raymond A., 20
Sorrentino, Gilbert, 28, 146
Speir, Jerry, 64, 81–82, 91, 93, 124, 126, 146
Spillane, Mickey, 25, 33, 62, 63
Stade, George, 144
Steele, Timothy, 22, 23, 144
Steiner, T. R., 20–21, 94, 109, 112–13, 146
Stowe, William W., 143
Svoboda, Frederic, 144
Symonds, Julian, 12, 146

Thirteen Steps, The (John Buchan), 36

Tomashevsky, Boris, 130
Track of the Cat, The (Walter Van Tilburg Clark), 21
Tutunjian, Jerry, 142

Van Meter, Jan R., 142

Warga, Wayne, 13
Welty, Eudora, 12, 20
West, Nathanael, 17
Wilson, Edmund, 30
Winks, Robbin W., 144
Wolfe, Peter, 65, 93, 136, 146

Young, 146